God's Plan for Christian Living

First Baptist, Jackson, Mississippi

Published by Innovo Publishing, LLC
www.innovopublishing.com
1-888-546-2111

Providing Full-Service Publishing Services for Christian Authors & Ministries:
Books, eBooks, Audiobooks, Music & Film

God's Plan for Christian Living

Copyright © 2018 First Baptist, Jackson, Mississippi
All rights reserved.

No part of this publication may be reproduced, stored in a retrieval system, or transmitted in any form or by any means electronic, mechanical, photocopying, recording, or otherwise, without the prior written permission of the author.

Good News Translation® (Today's English Version)
Copyright © 1976 American Bible Society. All rights reserved.

Library of Congress Control Number: 2018942677
ISBN: 978-1-61314-401-5

Cover Design & Interior Layout: Innovo Publishing, LLC

Printed in the United States of America
U.S. Printing History
First Edition: 1984
Second Edition: 2003
Third Edition: 2016
Fourth Edition: 2018

Endorsements

"I loved these lessons for teaching the Bible to those who have never heard or studied the Bible and seeing their hearts open to God's truth. Written in a simple, easy-to-use, and easy-to-understand format and yet so profound."

—Charlie and Nita, former teachers and directors of the Friend-to-Friend International Sunday School Department

"*God's Plan of Love* and *God's Plan for Christian Living* were each written one Monday at a time, getting the lesson ready for the following Sunday. Countless hours were spent in prayer, writing, editing, and proofreading. They are not deep theological books, but simple, practical introductions to God's amazing love to and for those who have never heard!"

—Becky, former director of the Friend-to-Friend International Ministry (week-day ministry and Sunday School Department) and one of the original authors

"The request for an endorsement of these two books has stirred many long-ago memories of afternoons around a dining room table, of fervent prayers for guidance, of knowledge gleaned from lifetimes of sermons and Sunday School lessons, of a feeling of being carried along by a Power far beyond ourselves. But mostly my memories are of the people around that table and of the contributions each person made to our collaborative effort. We were simply writing 'next Sunday's lesson.' We never dreamed that those lessons could or would be used for many years and in many places. Praise God!"

—Martha Jean, a long-time teacher in the Friend-to-Friend International Ministry and one of the original authors

"*God's Plan of Love* and *God's Plan for Christian Living* were written by a group of dedicated Christian women. The lessons are well written and Christ centered. As a teacher for many years, I found the two books to be excellent teaching guides for me."

—Clarice, a long-time and dedicated teacher in the Friend-to-Friend International Sunday School Department

Acknowledgments

(1984)

First Baptist, Jackson, Mississippi, and the writers of this material express grateful acknowledgment to the American Bible Society for use of the Good News Bible, both text and illustrations, c. 1976.

We wish to thank Anand Michael from India who is a member of First Baptist, Jackson, Mississippi, and the International Sunday School. His contribution of time and effort in making attractive posters, vocabulary cards, and sentence strips for teaching aids was priceless.

First Baptist, Jackson, Mississippi, would also like to acknowledge the invaluable contributions of Mrs. Frances Smira, WMU Director, and Mr. David Roddy, Minister of Education. Without their help, this publication would not have been possible.

To the people who prayed for the writers/teachers and the writings, we give sincere and humble thanks.

INTERNATIONAL DEPARTMENT: First Baptist, Jackson, Mississippi

Mrs. Winfred (Becky) Lott, Director: 1980-2001

Teachers:	**Associates:**
Mrs. Joel (Martha Jean) Alvis	Dr. Joel E. Alvis
Mrs. Tom (Mercedes) Cleveland	Miss Fidelia Campbell
Mrs. Roy (Ann) Moore	Mrs. Roy (Georgie) Collum
Mrs. Herbert (Margaret) Price	Winfred B. Lott
Mrs. Robert (Rene) Sugg	Robert (Bob) Smira
	Mrs. Bob (Frances) Smira

Contents

Foreword xi

Part I: The Beginning of the Christian Life

Lesson 1: *You Must Be Born Again (John 3:1-17)* 15

Lesson 2: *Know Who You Are* 18

Lesson 3: *Begin to Grow* 22

Lesson 4: *Study the Bible (Psalm 119)* 25

Lesson 5: *Family Bible Study* 28

Lesson 6: *Pray! Pray! Pray!* 31

Lesson 7: *Pray! Pray! Pray! (Continued)* 34

Part II: Christmas Celebration

Lesson 8: *God's Plan for Jesus to Come* 41

Lesson 9: *In the Right Time, Jesus Came* 44

Lesson 10: *Jesus Came to a Human Family* 47

Lesson 11: *The Christmas Story* 50

Lesson 12: *Looking Back, Looking Ahead* 57

Part III: The Christian Life—A New Kind of Living!

Lesson 13: *The Power in the Christian Life* 61

Lesson 14: *The Need for God's Power in the Christian Life* 63

Lesson 15: *Choosing the Fullness of God's Power* 65

Lesson 16: *The Result of God's Power in the Christian Life* 67

Lesson 17: *God Loves You* 69

Lesson 18: *God Loves You (Continued)* 71

Lesson 19: *God Tells You* 74

Lesson 20: *God Tells You (Continued)* 76

Contents

    Lesson 21: *God Tells You (Continued)* 78

    Lesson 22: *God Tells You (Continued)* 80

    Lesson 23: *God Tells You (Continued)* 82

    Lesson 24: *God Tells You (Continued)* 84

    Lesson 25: *God Tells You (Continued)* 86

Part IV: Easter Celebration—God's Plan Fulfilled

    Lesson 26: *Jesus' Special Supper with His Friends* 91

    Lesson 27: *Jesus in the Garden of Gethsemane* 94

    Lesson 28: *Jesus' Trial* 97

    Lesson 29: *Jesus' Death on the Cross* 101

    Lesson 30: *The Lord Is Risen!* 105

    Lesson 31: *Jesus' Last Days on Earth* 107

Part V: The Christian Life—Growing through Obedience

    Lesson 32: *Abraham Obeyed God* 113

    Lesson 33: *Abraham Trusted God When It Seemed Impossible* 115

    Lesson 34: *Abraham Obeyed God When It Seemed Impossible* 117

    Lesson 35: *Moses Obeyed God after Moses Made Excuses* 119

    Lesson 36: *Joshua Led the People to Obey God* 122

    Lesson 37: *Gideon Obeyed God When He Was Afraid* 124

    Lesson 38: *Saul Chose Not to Obey God* 126

    Lesson 39: *Elijah Obeyed God* 128

    Lesson 40: *Jonah Tried to Disobey God* 130

    Lesson 41: *Daniel Obeyed God* 132

    Lesson 42: *Esther Obeyed and God Saved Her People* 135

    Lesson 43: *Mary Chose to Obey God* 137

    Lesson 44: *Jesus Called, the Fishermen Obeyed* 139

    Lesson 45: *A Boy Who Obeyed* 141

    Lesson 46: *Paul Chose to Obey God* 143

    Lesson 47: *Jesus: The Perfect Example of Obedience* 145

Lesson 48: *Jesus: The Perfect Example of Obedience (Continued)* 147

Lesson 49: *Jesus: The Perfect Example of Obedience (Continued)* 149

Part VI: The Christian Life—Living as God's Dear Children

Lesson 50: *Living as God's Dear Children* 155

Lesson 51: *No More Lying!* 157

Lesson 52: *Do Not Stay Angry* 159

Lesson 53: *Do Not Stay Angry (Continued)* 162

Lesson 54: *God Will Help You* 164

Lesson 55: *Put on God's Armor* 166

Lesson 56: *Thank You, God!* 168

Lesson 57: *Relationships* 171

God's Plan for Christian Living

Foreword

The Bible study material included in *God's Plan of Love* and *God's Plan for Christian Living* was prepared initially for use with international adults* in a Sunday school setting. It was written for people with a limited knowledge of English. No background knowledge of the Bible was assumed.

Two principles were followed in writing the lessons: One was to present the thread of redemption from the creation of the world through the death, burial, resurrection, and ascension of Jesus, including two lessons giving the plan of salvation. The thread of redemption was also carried through the beginning of the church and the second coming of Jesus. The lessons stress the importance of choosing God's way (making a decision of faith in Jesus) and obedience.

The other principle in both volumes was to replace theological terms with simple, everyday words to teach spiritual truths.

This material was written as basic statements to be used as a guide, by which lessons could be prepared to teach people at different levels of English proficiency. Understanding on the part of the students was of more importance than strict adherence to accepted outline procedure.

Each lesson may be easily divided into shorter lessons when repetition and simplification are needed. On the other hand, each lesson, or portions thereof, can be taken to a more advanced English level by using the Bible itself to expand the details of the truth being taught, to raise the language level, and to introduce deeper concepts that might be needed.

The initial teaching of this material began in May 1984, with a natural progression of study planned to teach the birth of Jesus at Christmas and the death, burial, and resurrection during the Easter season. However, each of these special lessons can be taught whenever they occur in your schedule of classes or saved for Christmas and Easter, respectively.

The Good News Bible, c. 1976, was used as a textbook. Illustrations from the Good News Bible, c. 1976, were included in the original writing.

In this 2018 edition of *God's Plan of Love* and *God's Plan for Christian Living*, the quotations from the Good News Bible have been retained with spaces after each quotation for page numbers to be inserted to help those students who may be unfamiliar with the Bible. You

Foreword

will need to explain the variety of translations available today and why you have chosen the version you prefer to use.

The original authors of these lessons dedicated them to the glory of God. Others who have taught these lessons for more than thirty years pray that you who teach them today will be able to adapt and use them to bring many people to "the throne of grace" and for the glory of the God and Father of our Lord Jesus.

_____

* Beyond the express purpose for which *God's Plan of Love* and *God's Plan for Christian Living* were written—that is, for limited English speakers—we commend these lessons to all Bible teachers as suitable for study by native English speakers. New believers in Jesus Christ as well as Christians who may not be thoroughly familiar with the Bible would benefit greatly from studying the chronological presentation of the highlights of the Bible in simple English.

Part I:

The Beginning of the Christian Life

Part I: The Beginning of the Christian Life

Lesson 1

You Must Be Born Again (John 3:1-17)

Memory Verse: John 3:7 (page _____ in the New Testament): "Do not be surprised because I tell you that you must all be born again."

1. **A religious leader named Nicodemus went to talk to Jesus.**

   John 3:1-2 (page _____ in the New Testament): There was a Jewish leader named Nicodemus, who belonged to the party of the Pharisees. One night he went to Jesus and said to Him, "Rabbi, we know that You are a teacher sent by God. No one could perform the miracles You are doing unless God were with Him."

2. **Jesus told Nicodemus that everyone must be born again.**

   John 3:3 (page _____ in the New Testament): Jesus answered, "I am telling you the truth: no one can see the Kingdom of God unless he is born again."

3. **Nicodemus did not understand about being "born again."**

   John 3:4 (page _____ in the New Testament): "How can a grown man be born again?"

4. **Jesus told Nicodemus that each person is born physically of human parents. Each person can choose to be born again by God's Spirit.**

   John 3:5-8 (page _____ in the New Testament): "I am telling you the truth," Jesus replied, "that no one can enter the Kingdom of God unless he is born of water and the Spirit. A person is born physically of human parents, but he is born spiritually of the Spirit. Do not be surprised because I tell you that you must all be born again. The wind blows

God's Plan for Christian Living

wherever it wishes; you hear the sound it makes, but you do not know where it comes from or where it is going. It is like that with everyone who is born of the Spirit."

John 3:9 (page ____ in the New Testament): "How can this be?" asked Nicodemus.

5. **The new birth/born again cannot be fully explained with words. The new birth/born again can be understood only through a personal experience.**

   John 3:10-13 (page ____ in the New Testament): Jesus answered, "You are a great teacher in Israel, and you don't know this? I am telling you the truth: we speak of what we know and report what we have seen, yet none of you is willing to accept our message. You do not believe Me when I tell you about the things of this world; how will you ever believe Me, then, when I tell you about the things of heaven? And no one has ever gone up to heaven except the Son of Man, who came down from heaven."

6. **Jesus told Nicodemus a story from the Old Testament. He told how the children of Israel were healed when they believed God.**

   Numbers 21:4-9 (page ____ in the Old Testament).

7. **Jesus also told Nicodemus that everyone who believes in Him will have eternal life. When a person is born again, he has eternal life.**

   John 3:14-15 (page ____ in the New Testament): "As Moses lifted up the bronze snake on a pole in the desert, in the same way the Son of Man must be lifted up, so that everyone who believes in Him may have eternal life."

8. **Eternal life is God's gift because of His love.**
   - Eternal life begins when a person is born again.
   - Eternal life gives God's love, joy, and peace now.
   - Eternal life is living forever with God.

   John 3:16 (page ____ in the New Testament): For God loved the world so much that He gave His only Son, so that everyone who believes in Him may not die but have eternal life.

Living the Christian life begins when you are born again.

Part I: The Beginning of the Christian Life

> *Have you been born again?*
>
> *You are born again when you choose God's way.*
>
> *You choose God's way when you believe in God and believe that Jesus is God's Son.*
>
> *Ask Jesus to come into your life, and obey Him.*

Write your answer to each of the questions below (yes or no):

1. Have you chosen God's way? _____

2. Have you asked Jesus to come into your life? _____

3. Do you want to obey God? _____

4. If you have not chosen God's way, you can choose now. Will you choose God's way now? _____

Lesson 2:

Know Who You Are

> *Memory Verse: 2 Corinthians 5:17 (page _____ in the New Testament): When anyone is joined to Christ, he is a new being; the old is gone, the new has come.*

Choosing God's way for your life means:

- to believe in God,
- to believe that Jesus is God's Son, and
- to ask Jesus to come into your life and obey Him.

Living the Christian life begins when you choose God's way for your life. Living the Christian life begins when you are born again.

1. **You are a new person.**

   2 Corinthians 5:17 (page _____ in the New Testament): When anyone is joined to Christ, he is a new being; the old is gone, the new has come.

   i. You are forgiven.

      Colossians 2:13b-14 (page _____ in the New Testament): But God has now brought you to life with Christ. God forgave us all our sins; He canceled the unfavorable record of our debts with its binding rules and did away with it completely by nailing it to the cross.

   ii. God/Jesus Christ/the Holy Spirit lives within you.

      Colossians 1:27 (page _____ in the New Testament): God's plan is to make known His secret to His people, this rich and glorious secret which He has for all peoples. And the secret is that Christ is in you, which means that you will share in the glory of God.

Part I: The Beginning of the Christian Life

    iii. You have access to God.

    Ephesians 3:12 (page _____ in the New Testament): In union with Christ and through our faith in Him we have the boldness to go into God's presence with all confidence.

    iv. Nothing can separate us from the love of God.

    Romans 8:37-39 (page _____ in the New Testament): No, in all these things we have complete victory through Him who loved us! For I am certain that nothing can separate us from His love: neither death nor life, neither angels nor other heavenly rulers or powers, neither the present nor the future, neither the world above nor the world below—there is nothing in all creation that will ever be able to separate us from the love of God which is ours through Christ Jesus our Lord.

2. **You have a new family.**

   Ephesians 2:19 (page _____ in the New Testament): So then, you Gentiles are not foreigners or strangers any longer; you are now fellow citizens with God's people and members of the family of God.

   i. You can call God "Father."

   Romans 8:14-15 (page _____ in the New Testament): Those who are led by God's Spirit are God's sons. For the Spirit that God has given you does not make you slaves and cause you to be afraid; instead, the Spirit makes you God's children, and by the Spirit's power we cry out to God, "Father! my Father!"

   ii. All Christians are your brothers and sisters in Christ.

   Romans 8:16-17 (page _____ in the New Testament): God's Spirit joins Himself to our spirits to declare that we are God's children. Since we are His children, we will possess the blessings He keeps for His people, and we will also possess with Christ what God has kept for Him; for if we share Christ's suffering, we will also share His glory. (Read Romans 16, page _____ in the New Testament.)

3. **You have new resources for living every day.**

   John 14:16 (page _____ in the New Testament): "I will ask the Father, and He will give you another Helper, who will stay with you forever."

   i. God's presence.

   Matthew 28:20b (page _____ in the New Testament): "And I will be with you always, to the end of the age."

   ii. God's power.

   Acts 1:8 (page _____ in the New Testament): "But when the Holy Spirit comes upon you, you will be filled with power, and you will be witnesses for Me in Jerusalem, in all Judea and Samaria, and to the ends of the earth."

iii. God's peace.

   John 14:27 (page _____ in the New Testament): "Peace is what I leave with you; it is My own peace that I give you. I do not give it as the world does. Do not be worried and upset; do not be afraid."

iv. God's viewpoint.

   Matthew 6:31-34 (page _____ in the New Testament): "So do not start worrying: 'Where will my food come from? or my drink? or my clothes?' (These are the things the pagans are always concerned about.) Your Father in heaven knows that you need all these things. Instead, be concerned above everything else with the Kingdom of God and with what He requires of you, and He will provide you with all these other things. So do not worry about tomorrow; it will have enough worries of its own. There is no need to add to the troubles each day brings."

4. You have a new purpose for your life.

2 Corinthians 6:16b–6:18 (page _____ in the New Testament): For we are the temple of the living God! As God Himself has said, "I will make my home with My people and live among them; I will be their God, and they shall be My people." And so the Lord says, "You must leave them and separate yourselves from them. Have nothing to do with what is unclean, and I will accept you. I will be your Father, and you shall be My sons and daughters," says the Lord Almighty.

All these promises are made to us, my dear friends. So then, let us purify ourselves from everything that makes body or soul unclean, and let us be completely holy by living in awe of God.

You became a Christian—a new person—by accepting Jesus Christ.

Every day you live as a Christian—a new person—by knowing who you are.

Every day you live as a Christian—a new person—by using these resources from God in your life.

Answer the following questions:

1. Who are you?
   _____

2. Who is your new family?
   _____

3. What resources do you have to help you live as a Christian every day?
   _____
   _____
   _____

Lesson 3

Begin to Grow

Memory Verse: 1 John 3:18 (page _____ in the New Testament): My children, our love should not be just words and talk; it must be true love, which shows itself in action.

When you have chosen God's way for your life, when you have been born again, you are a CHRISTIAN!

Newborn babies need to grow. Their bodies need to become bigger and stronger. Their minds need to develop. Physical growth and mental development need to happen every day. Growth and development continue throughout life.

Newborn Christians need to grow in the Christian life. Newborn Christians need to grow in the Christian life every day. Christian growth needs to continue throughout the Christian's life. In order to grow in the Christian life...

1. **If possible, tell someone that you have asked Jesus to come into your life.**

    Mark 5:19 (page _____ in the New Testament): Jesus ... told him, "Go back home to your family and tell them how much the Lord has done for you and how kind He has been to you."

2. **Begin to study the Bible every day.**

    Psalm 119:105 (page _____ in the Old Testament): Your Word is a lamp to guide me and a light for my path.

3. Begin to talk with God and pray every day.

Jeremiah 33:2-3 (page _____ in the Old Testament): The LORD, who made the earth, who formed it and set it in place, spoke to me. He whose name is the LORD said, "Call to Me, and I will answer you; I will tell you wonderful and marvelous things that you know nothing about."

4. Become a part of a group of Christians. Join a church. Members of a church…

i. Study the Bible together.

Acts 17:11b (page _____ in the New Testament): They listened to the message with great eagerness, and every day they studied the Scriptures to see if what Paul said was really true.

ii. Worship together.

Colossians 3:16 (page _____ in the New Testament): Christ's message in all its richness must live in your hearts. Teach and instruct one another with all wisdom. Sing psalms, hymns, and sacred songs; sing to God with thanksgiving in your hearts.

iii. Tell the Good News of God's love around the world.

Acts 1:8 (page _____ in the New Testament): "But when the Holy Spirit comes upon you, you will be filled with power, and you will be witnesses for Me in Jerusalem, in all of Judea and Samaria, and to the ends of the earth."

iv. Help each other.

Hebrews 10:24 (page _____ in the New Testament): Let us be concerned for one another, to help one another to show love and to do good.

Acts 2:42, 46-47 (page _____ in the New Testament): They spent their time in learning from the apostles, taking part in the fellowship, and sharing in the fellowship meals and the prayers . . . .Day after day they met as a group in the Temple, and they had their meals together in their homes, eating with glad and humble hearts praising God, and enjoying the goodwill of all the people. And every day the Lord added to their group those who were being saved.

5. If possible, be baptized.

Romans 6:4 (page _____ in the New Testament): By our baptism, then, we were buried with Him and shared His death, in order that, just as Christ was raised from death by the glorious power of the Father, so also we might live a new life.

God's Plan for Christian Living

6. Show God's love in your daily life.

1 John 3:18 (page _____ in the New Testament): My children, our love should not be just words and talk; it must be true love, which shows itself in action.

> **Our conduct is a statement of the life we now have in**
>
> **Christ Jesus.**
>
> **All that we do should give glory to God.**

This lesson tells six ways to grow in the Christian life. Write the six ways:

1. _____

2. _____

3. _____

4. _____

5. _____

6. _____

Will you choose at least one way that will help you to grow this week?
Write your choice here:

_____
_____
_____
_____

Part I: The Beginning of the Christian Life

Lesson 4

Study the Bible (Psalm 119)

Memory Verse: Psalm 119:105 (page _____ in the Old Testament): Your Word is a lamp to guide me and a light for my path.

Daily Bible study and prayer are essential for a Christian to grow in the Christian life.

The Bible is God's Word for people today. The Bible tells people God's truths. The Bible tells people how to live God's way.

Some suggestions for beginning to read your Bible each day are...

1. **Ask God to help you begin your Bible study.**

    Psalm 119:12 (page _____ in the Old Testament): I praise You, O LORD; teach me Your ways.

2. **If possible, decide on a definite time and place for studying the Bible.**

    Psalm 119:147 (page _____ in the Old Testament): Before sunrise I call to You for help; I place my hope in Your promise.

    Psalm 119:55 (page _____ in the Old Testament): In the night I remember You, LORD, and I think about Your law.

3. **Follow a plan for studying the Bible.**

    Psalm 119:23b-24 (page _____ in the Old Testament): I will study Your teachings. Your instructions give me pleasure; they are my advisers.

4. **Each day, ask God to help you understand what you are studying.**

    Psalm 119:144 (page _____ in the Old Testament): Your instructions are always just; give me understanding, and I shall live.

God's Plan for Christian Living

5. Read the part of the Bible decided on for today.

Psalm 119:15 (page _____ in the Old Testament): I study Your instructions; I examine Your teachings.

6. Think about what you have read.

Psalm 119:11 (page _____ in the Old Testament): I keep Your law in my heart, so that I will not sin against You.

7. Ask God to remind you often of what you have studied.

Psalm 119:97 (page _____ in the Old Testament): How I love Your law! I think about it all day long.

8. Thank God for His message for you each day.

Psalm 119:108 (page _____ in the Old Testament): Accept my prayer of thanks, O LORD, and teach me Your commands.

Some suggestions for your personal Bible study are . . .

1. Use Bible readings listed at the end of each Sunday school lesson.

2. Pray.

3. _____

4. _____

5. _____

> *Psalm 119:47-48 (page _____ in the Old Testament): I find pleasure in obeying Your commands, because I love them. I respect and love Your commandments; I will meditate on Your instructions.*

Part I: The Beginning of the Christian Life

> *Every day I will have a personal Bible study.*
>
> *My name*_____
>
> *Place*_____
>
> *Time*_____

DAILY BIBLE READINGS—Read from the Bible in your language and from the Good News Bible/Sunday School Bible:

Sunday	Psalm 119:29-32
Monday	Psalm 119:63-64
Tuesday	Psalm 119:73-74
Wednesday	Psalm 119:90-91
Thursday	Psalm 119:132-134
Friday	Psalm 119:159-160
Saturday	Psalm 119:166-168

Lesson 5

Family Bible Study

> *Memory Verse: Colossians 3:16 (page _____ in the New Testament): Christ's message in all its richness must live in your hearts. Teach and instruct one another with all wisdom. Sing psalms, hymns, and sacred songs; sing to God with thanksgiving in your hearts.*

Daily Bible study and prayer are essential for a Christian to grow in the Christian life.

1. **God made the family. God chose the family to show His plan of love.**

   Genesis 1:27-28a (page _____ in the Old Testament): So God created human beings, making them to be like Himself. He created them male and female, blessed them, and said, "Have many children, so that your descendants will live all over the earth and bring it under their control."

2. **God chose parents to teach their children His plan of love. God wanted parents to teach their children about Him. He wanted parents and children to know His Word. Teaching the Bible at home helps children to learn to:**

   i. love and obey God,

   ii. love and obey parents, and

   iii. love and obey people in authority (teachers, officers of the law, government officials).

   Deuteronomy 6:5-7 (page _____ in the Old Testament): "Love the LORD your God with all your heart, with all your soul, and with all your strength. Never forget these commands that I am giving you today. Teach them to your children. Repeat them when you are at home and when you are away, when you are resting and when you are working."

3. God wants parents and children to know all of His Word.

2 Timothy 3:14-17 (page ____ in the New Testament): But as for you, continue in the truths that you were taught and firmly believe. You know who your teachers were, and you remember that ever since you were a child, you have known the Holy Scriptures, which are able to give you the wisdom that leads to salvation through faith in Christ Jesus. All Scripture is inspired by God and is useful for teaching the truth, rebuking error, correcting faults, and giving instruction for right living so that the person who serves God may be fully qualified and equipped to do every kind of good deed.

Here are some suggestions for your family Bible study:

i. Decide to have a Bible study. Make it a happy time to think of God.

ii. Choose a time and place.

iii. Choose a plan. Your plan might include some of these:

- *Read the Bible.*
- *Pray.*
- *Sing songs of praise.*
- *Read from a devotional book.*
- *Quote memory verses that have been memorized.*

iv. Teach the children to live all through the day by what they have learned in family Bible study.

> *Deuteronomy 11:19 (page ____ in the Old Testament): "Teach [God's laws] to your children. Talk about them when you are at home and when you are away, when you are resting and when you are working."*

Every day our family will have a family Bible study.

Name _____

Place _____

Time _____

DAILY BIBLE READINGS—Read from the Bible in your language and from the Good News Bible/Sunday School Bible:

Sunday	1 Corinthians 13:4-7
Monday	1 Corinthians 13:4-7
Tuesday	1 Corinthians 13:4-7
Wednesday	1 Corinthians 13:4-7
Thursday	1 Corinthians 13:4-7
Friday	1 Corinthians 13:4-7
Saturday	1 Corinthians 13:4-7

Part I: The Beginning of the Christian Life

Lesson 6

Pray! Pray! Pray!

Memory Verse: Jeremiah 33:2-3 (page _____ in the Old Testament): The LORD, who made the earth, who formed it and set it in place, spoke to me. He whose name is the LORD said, "Call to Me, and I will answer you; I will tell you wonderful and marvelous things that you know nothing about."

Daily Bible study and prayer are essential for a Christian to grow in the Christian life.

- Prayer is communication between God and people.
- Prayer is a special way people express love for God.
- Prayer is a special way people tell God about their needs.
- Prayer is a special way God teaches people about His love.
- Prayer is getting to know God.

For Christians, prayer is communication with God through Jesus Christ.

1. **You can pray:**

    i. With your own words in your own language.

    ii. With words of other people:

    "Lord, give me the courage to change what can be changed, the patience to accept what cannot be changed, and the wisdom to know the difference."

    iii. With words of hymns:

    "Into my heart, come into my heart, Lord Jesus. Come in today; come in to stay, Come into my heart, Lord Jesus."

God's Plan for Christian Living

iv. With words of the Bible:

   Psalm 23 (page _____ in the Old Testament): The LORD is my shepherd; I have everything I need. He lets me rest in fields of green grass and leads me to quiet pools of fresh water. He gives me new strength. He guides me in the right paths, as he has promised. Even if I go through the deepest darkness, I will not be afraid, LORD, for You are with me. Your shepherd's rod and staff protect me. You prepare a banquet for me where all my enemies can see me; You welcome me as an honored guest and fill my cup to the brim. I know that Your goodness and love will be with me all my life; and Your house will be my home as long as I live.

2. **You can pray alone.**

   Matthew 6:6 (page _____ in the New Testament): "But when you pray, go to your room, close the door, and pray to your Father, who is unseen. And your Father, who sees what you do in private, will reward you."

3. **You can pray with other people in your home, in groups, in church.**

   Matthew 18:20 (page _____ in the New Testament): "For where two or three come together in My name, I am there with them."

4. **You can pray:**

   i. To glorify/praise God.

   Ephesians 1:6 (page _____ in the New Testament): Let us praise God for His glorious grace, for the free gift He gave us in His dear Son!

   ii. To feel God's presence.

   Psalm 116:1-2 (page _____ in the Old Testament): I love the LORD because He hears me; He listens to my prayers. He listens to me every time I call to Him.

   iii. For comfort in time of need.

   2 Corinthians 1:3-4 (page _____ in the New Testament): Let us give thanks to the God and Father of our Lord Jesus Christ, the merciful Father, the God from whom all help comes! He helps us in all our troubles so that we are able to help others who have all kinds of troubles, using the same help that we ourselves have received from God.

   iv. To experience God's forgiveness.

   Psalm 51:1-4, 7, 9-10 (page _____ in the Old Testament): Be merciful to me, O God, because of Your constant love. Because of Your great mercy wipe away my sins! Wash away all my evil and make me clean from my sin! I recognize my faults; I am always conscious of my sins. I have sinned against You—only against You—and done what You consider evil. So You are right in judging me; You are justified in condemning me . . . . Remove my sin, and I will be clean; wash me, and I will be whiter than snow . . . . Close your eyes to my sins and wipe out all my evil. Create a pure heart in me, O God, and put a new and loyal spirit in me.

Part I: The Beginning of the Christian Life

    v. To know God's guidance and direction.

Psalm 25:4-5 (page _____ in the Old Testament): Teach me Your ways, O LORD; make them known to me. Teach me to live according to Your truth, for You are my God, Who saves me. I always trust in You.

Psalm 32:8 (page _____ in the Old Testament): The LORD says, "I will teach you the way you should go; I will instruct you and advise you."

    vi. To resist temptation.

Ephesians 6:13 (page _____ in the New Testament): So put on God's armor now! Then when the evil day comes, you will be able to resist the enemy's attacks; and after fighting to the end, you will still hold your ground.

5. You can pray anywhere, anytime!

Ephesians 6:18 (page _____ in the New Testament): Do all this in prayer, asking for God's help. Pray on every occasion, as the Spirit leads. For this reason, keep alert and never give up; pray always for all God's people.

Some suggestions to include in your daily prayers are the following:

- Sunday: Thank God for your family.
- Monday: Pray for the people of your native country.
- Tuesday: Pray for the people of the United States of America.
- Wednesday: Pray for wisdom for the leaders of all the countries of the world.
- Thursday: Pray for the people in your neighborhood.
- Friday: Pray for your children and their friends.
- Saturday: Pray for the people in your Sunday School class, the Sunday School teachers, and the pastor of the church.

DAILY BIBLE READINGS—Read from the Bible in your language and from the Good News Bible/Sunday School Bible:

Sunday	Ephesians 5:33–6:4
Monday	Psalm 33:8-12
Tuesday	Psalm 33:13-15
Wednesday	1 Timothy 2:1-2
Thursday	Proverbs 3:27-30
Friday	Proverbs 3:5-7
Saturday	Philemon 4-7

Lesson 7

Pray! Pray! Pray! (Continued)

Memory Verse: Jeremiah 33:2-3 (page _____ in the Old Testament): The LORD, who made the earth, who formed it and set it in place, spoke to me. He whose name is the LORD said, "Call to Me, and I will answer you; I will tell you wonderful and marvelous things that you know nothing about."

*Prayer is getting to know God through Jesus Christ.
Prayer is realizing your need for Jesus Christ.
Prayer is recognizing His/God's presence in your life.*

*You learn to pray by praying.
You can talk to God anywhere, at any time, in any language.
You can tell God just what you think.
You can tell God just how you feel.*

God does answer your prayers!

Sometimes God's answer is, "Yes."

Sometimes God's answer is, "No."

Sometimes God's answer is, "Wait."

1. **Some things in your life keep you from praying:**

    i. An unforgiving spirit.

    Mark 11:25 (page _____ in the New Testament): "And when you stand and pray, forgive anything you may have against anyone, so that your Father in heaven will forgive the wrongs you have done."

    ii. Unconfessed sin.

    Psalm 66:18 (page _____ in the Old Testament): If I had ignored my sins, the Lord would not have listened to me.

    iii. Disobeying God.

    Ephesians 2:1 (page _____ in the New Testament): In the past, you were spiritually dead because of your disobedience and sins.

    Titus 3:3a (page _____ in the New Testament): For we ourselves were once foolish, disobedient, and wrong.

    iv. Being too busy.

    Luke 8:14 (page _____ in the New Testament): "The seeds that fell among thorn bushes stand for those who hear; but the worries and riches and pleasures of this life crowd in and choke them, and their fruit never ripens."

2. **Some things in your life help you to pray:**

    i. A forgiving spirit.

    Matthew 6:14-15 (page _____ in the New Testament): "If you forgive others the wrongs they have done to you, your Father in heaven will also forgive you. But if you do not forgive others, then your Father will not forgive the wrongs you have done."

    ii. Confessed sin.

    1 John 1:8-10 (page _____ in the New Testament): If we say that we have no sin, we deceive ourselves, and there is no truth in us. But if we confess our sins to God, He will keep His promise and do what is right: He will forgive us our sins and purify us from all our wrongdoing. If we say that we have not sinned, we make a liar out of God, and His word is not in us.

    iii. Obeying God.

    1 Peter 1:14 (page _____ in the New Testament): Be obedient to God, and do not allow your lives to be shaped by those desires you had when you were still ignorant.

iv. A quiet time.

Psalm 46:10a (page _____ in the Old Testament KJV): Be still and know that I am God . . . .

Ephesians 3:17-18 (page _____ in the New Testament): . . . .and I pray that Christ will make His home in your hearts through faith. I pray that you may have your roots and foundation in love, so that you, together with all God's people, may have the power to understand how broad and long, how high and deep, is Christ's love.

3. Your prayers can include:

PRAISE: Telling God that He is great, glorious, wonderful, marvelous and that you love Him.

"God, You are . . . _____

_____."

THANKSGIVING: Thanking God for all things.

"Dear God, thank You for . . . _____

_____."

CONFESSION: Telling God about my sins and asking His forgiveness.

"Father in heaven, I know I have thought bad things, I have said bad things, and I have done bad things. Please forgive me for . . .

_____

_____."

PETITION: Asking God for all my needs.

"Father, I need . . . _____

_____."

INTERCESSION: Praying for all people, including my family, people in authority, and my enemies.

"Dear Father in heaven, I pray for . . . _____

_____."

GUIDANCE: Asking God to help me obey Him in every way, every day.

"*Dear Lord, I need Your help for . . .* _____
_____."

DAILY BIBLE READINGS—Read from the Bible in your language and from the Good News Bible/Sunday School Bible:

Sunday	Romans 8:28
Monday	Matthew 7:7-11
Tuesday	2 Corinthians 12:8-10
Wednesday	Hebrews 10:36-39
Thursday	Isaiah 43:1-5
Friday	Isaiah 12:1-3
Saturday	Isaiah 12:4-6

Part II:

Christmas Celebration

Part II: Christmas Celebration

Lesson 8

God's Plan for Jesus to Come

Memory Verse: John 1:14 (page _____ in the New Testament): The Word became a human being, and full of grace and truth, lived among us. We saw His glory, the glory which He received as the Father's only Son.

Christmas is the celebration of the birth of Jesus. God had promised for many years that Jesus would be born. God prepared a special family for Jesus. God prepared this family for many generations. The Bible tells us about this family. The ancestors of Jesus are named in Matthew 1:1-16 (page _____ in the New Testament).

Three ancestors of Jesus were Abraham, Ruth, and David. Abraham was the father of the national family of Jesus. Ruth was not a member of the national family. David was king of the national family through which the King of Kings/Jesus came.

Abraham was one of the ancestors of Jesus. God made a special promise to Abraham. God said to Abraham, "Through one of your descendants I will bless all nations."

Genesis 12:1-4 (page _____ in the Old Testament): The LORD said to Abram, "Leave your country, your relatives, and your father's home, and go to a land that I am going to show you. I will give you many descendants, and they will become a great nation. I will bless you and make your name famous, so that you will be a blessing. I will bless those who bless you, but I will curse those who curse you. And through you I will bless all the nations." When Abram was seventy-five years old, he started out from Haran, as the LORD had told him to do.

Abraham believed God would keep His promise. He obeyed what God told him to do. God kept His promise to Abraham through his son Isaac. God kept His promise to Abraham through Jesus Christ, even though Jesus was born hundreds of years after Abraham died.

Galatians 3:16-17a (page _____ in the New Testament): Now, God made His promises to Abraham and to his descendant. The Scripture does not use the plural "descendants," meaning many people, but the singular "descendant," meaning one person only, namely, Christ. What I mean is that God made a covenant with Abraham and promised to keep it.

Ruth was one of the ancestors of Jesus. She was a part of God's plan of love.

Matthew 1:1-6a (page _____ in the New Testament): This is the list of the ancestors of Jesus Christ, a descendant of David, who was a descendant of Abraham. From Abraham to King David, the following ancestors are listed: . . . Salmon, Boaz (his mother was Rahab), Obed (his mother was Ruth), Jesse, and King David.

Ruth left her home in Moab to live with her mother-in-law, Naomi. Ruth's husband was dead, but she still wanted to live with Naomi. Ruth believed in the God of Naomi— the God of Abraham and the Israelites. Ruth married Boaz. Boaz was an Israelite. He was of the family of Abraham. He and Ruth had a son, Obed. Obed was the father of Jesse, and Jesse was the father of David. You can read about Ruth in the book of Ruth (page _____ in the Old Testament).

Ruth was an important person among the ancestors of Jesus Christ. She was a woman and a foreigner. She was not an Israelite. God chose to name Ruth as an ancestor of Jesus. He wanted to show His love for all people. He wanted to show His love for women. He wanted to show the importance of women in His plan of love.

In Ruth 1:16 (page _____ in the Old Testament): Ruth answered, "Don't ask me to leave you! Let me go with you. Wherever you go, I will go; wherever you live, I will live. Your people will be my people, and your God will be my God."

David was one of the ancestors of Jesus. God made a promise to David.

2 Samuel 7:16 (page _____ in the Old Testament): "You will always have descendants, and I will make your kingdom last forever. Your dynasty will never end."

Paul said in Acts 13:22b-23 (page _____ in the New Testament): God made David their (Israelites) king. This is what God said about him: "I have found that David, son of Jesse, is the kind of man I like, a man who will do all I want him to do." It was Jesus, a descendant of David, whom God made the Savior of the people of Israel, as He had promised.

Jesus said in Revelation 22:16 (page _____ in the New Testament): "I, Jesus, have sent My angel to announce these things to you in the churches. I am descended from the family of David; I am the bright morning star."

Part II: Christmas Celebration

God had a plan for Jesus to be born. Many people were part of God's plan. His plan took many years to be fulfilled.

God's plan is for every person to choose His way of life. Sometimes it takes many years for us to know God's plan for our lives. Do you understand God's plan for your life? Did it take many years for you to understand God's plan? Did God use many people to help you understand His plan?

You can know God's plan for your life. God tells His plan in John 3:16 (page ____ in the New Testament):

For God loved the world so much that He gave His only Son, so that everyone who believes in Him may not die but have eternal life.

DAILY BIBLE READINGS—Read from the Bible in your language and from the Good News Bible/Sunday School Bible:

Sunday	Hebrews 11:1-3
Monday	Hebrews 11:8-12
Tuesday	Genesis 17:7-8, 15-16
Wednesday	Ruth 1:15-19
Thursday	Ruth 2:10-12
Friday	Isaiah 11:1-5
Saturday	2 Samuel 23:1-5

Lesson 9

In the Right Time, Jesus Came

> *Memory Verse: Ecclesiastes 3:1 (page _____ in the Old Testament): Everything that happens in the world happens at the time God chooses.*
>
> *Galatians 4:4-5 (page _____ in the New Testament): But when the right time finally came, God sent His own Son. He came as the Son of a human mother and lived under the Jewish Law, to redeem those who were under the Law, so that we might become God's sons.*

1. **God's plan for Jesus:**

   1 Peter 1:19-20 (page _____ in the New Testament): It was the costly sacrifice of Christ, who was like a lamb without defect or flaw. He had been chosen by God before the creation of the world and was revealed in these last days for your sake.

   The Bible says: God is love. His love has no beginning and no end. God was Love before He made the world and the people in it. God had a plan to love people and for people to love Him even before He made people. God's plan was to come as a person, Jesus Christ. God's plan was to be born into a Jewish family, to die on the cross, to rise from the dead. His plan was for Jesus to pay for the sin of all the people in all of the world.

2. **God's plan for people:**

   Ephesians 1:4-5 (page _____ in the New Testament): Even before the world was made, God had already chosen us to be His through our union with Christ, so that we would be holy and without fault before Him. Because of His love God had already decided that through Jesus Christ He would make us His sons—this was His pleasure and purpose.

   God had a plan for people to love Him and to believe in Him. He had a plan for people to live forever with Him. God's plan was for people to walk and talk with

Him. God's plan was for people to be His friends. He had this plan before He made the world. His plan is for us today.

God's plan is for people to be holy. Holy means to be different, to be set aside for God. Set aside means to be special. The only way people can be holy is to believe that Jesus is God's Son and that He died for their sin.

God is without fault. God's plan is for people to be without fault. Without fault means without sin. The only way people can be with God is to be without sin. The only way people can be without sin is to believe that Jesus is God's Son and that He died for their sin.

God is love. Love was God's reason for His plan. He loved us before He made the world. He wants people to be with Him and to love Him.

3. God's plan for the right time:

   God chose the family for Jesus to be born into. Mary was His mother, and God was His Father. God gave Joseph to help Mary and Jesus.

   God chose the place for Jesus to be born. The place was Bethlehem.

   God chose the right time for Jesus to be born:

   i. There was peace in most of the world.
   ii. There were roads for people to travel from one country to another.
   iii. There were trade routes all over the world—Scotland to Southeast Asia, Africa to China.
   iv. There were one or two languages understood by many of the people.

The Good News of Jesus could be told all over the world.

Before sin was in our hearts, forgiveness was in God's heart.

At the right time—Jesus came!

God's Plan for Christian Living

Did something happen in your life at the right time? What was it? Write about it here:

_____

_____

_____

> God's plan is for you today. Have you chosen His plan for your life? If you have not, NOW is the best time for you to choose God's plan. If you choose God's plan today, write your name here:
>
> _____

> If you have chosen God's plan, will you tell His plan to someone you know? Write the name of that person here:
>
> _____

DAILY BIBLE READINGS—Read from the Bible in your language and from the Good News Bible/Sunday School Bible:

Sunday	Ecclesiastes 3:1-3
Monday	Galatians 4:4-5
Tuesday	1 Peter 1:18-20
Wednesday	Isaiah 53:5-8
Thursday	Ephesians 1:4-5
Friday	2 Peter 3:8-9
Saturday	Philippians 2:6-11

Part II: Christmas Celebration

Lesson 10

Jesus Came to a Human Family

Memory Verse: Matthew 1:18 (page _____ in the New Testament): This was how the birth of Jesus Christ took place. His mother Mary was engaged to Joseph, but before they were married, she found out that she was going to have a baby by the Holy Spirit.

God loves families. Families are a part of God's plan for people. God planned for the first people He made to live as a family. His plan today is for people to live as families. He wants people in a family to love one another.

God planned the human family for Jesus' birth. Mary was His mother, and God was His Father. God made Joseph to be the head of the family.

1. **God chose Mary to be the mother of Jesus. God sent an angel to tell Mary His plan for her life.**

   Luke 1:30-35, 37-38 (page _____ in the New Testament): The angel said to her, "Don't be afraid, Mary; God has been gracious to you. You will become pregnant and give birth to a son, and you will name Him Jesus. He will be great and will be called the Son of the Most High God. The Lord God will make Him a king, as His ancestor David was, and He will be the king of the descendants of Jacob forever; His kingdom will never end!" Mary said to the angel, "I am a virgin. How, then, can this be?" The angel answered, "The Holy Spirit will come on you, and God's power will rest upon you. For this reason, the holy child will be called the Son of God . . . . For there is nothing that God cannot do." "I am the Lord's servant," said Mary; "May it happen to me as you have said." And the angel left her.

2. **God's plan was for Jesus to be God in a human body.**

47

God's Plan for Christian Living

3. **God's plan was for Jesus to have a human mother without a human father. The Spirit of God would make this miracle happen.**

4. **Mary chose to obey God's plan for her life.**

    - Choosing God's plan could have meant that Mary would lose her reputation.
    - Choosing God's plan could have meant that Mary would not be married.
    - Choosing God's plan could have meant that Mary would be killed.
    - The Jewish law said a woman who had a baby without a husband must be killed.

    Mary understood what choosing God's plan could mean in her life. She obeyed God and chose His plan.

5. **God chose Joseph to be head of the human family of Jesus. God sent an angel to tell Joseph God's plan for his life. God's plan was for Joseph to marry Mary and take care of the family.**

    Matthew 1:19-25 (page _____ in the New Testament): Joseph was a man who always did what was right, but he did not want to disgrace Mary publicly; so he made plans to break the engagement privately. While he was thinking about this, an angel of the Lord appeared to him in a dream and said, "Joseph, descendant of David, do not be afraid to take Mary to be your wife. For it is by the Holy Spirit that she has conceived. She will have a son, and you will name Him Jesus—because He will save His people from their sins." Now all this happened in order to make come true what the Lord had said through the prophet, "A virgin will become pregnant and have a son, and He will be called Immanuel" (which means, "God is with us"). So when Joseph woke up, he married Mary, as the angel of the Lord had told him to. But he had no sexual relations with her before she gave birth to her son. And Joseph named Him Jesus.

6. **Joseph chose God's plan. Joseph married Mary. They did not live together as husband and wife before Jesus was born.**

    - Choosing God's plan meant he could lose his reputation.
    - Choosing God's plan meant that Joseph had faith in God and that he believed that Mary had been true to him.
    - Joseph obeyed God and chose His plan.

Today, choosing God's plan can mean:

- A person is rejected by his family.
- A person is rejected by his friends.
- A person loses his job.

In some places, choosing God's plan can mean a person will lose his life.

What would it mean for you to choose God's plan for your life? Choosing God's plan for your life ALWAYS means:

- God lives within you now.
- God's power is available to you now.
- You can live a victorious life.

> *Choosing God's plan for your life means that you will live forever with God!*

DAILY BIBLE READINGS—Read from the Bible in your language and from the Good News Bible/Sunday School Bible:

Sunday	Ephesians 1:4-5
Monday	Luke 1:28-33
Tuesday	Luke 1:38, 46-50
Wednesday	Luke 1:54-55
Thursday	Matthew 1:18-21
Friday	Matthew 1:22-25
Saturday	John 3:16-17

Lesson 11

The Christmas Story

> *Memory Verse: Isaiah 9:6 (page ____ in the Old Testament): A child is born to us! A son is given to us! And He will be our ruler. He will be called, "Wonderful Counselor," "Mighty God," "Eternal Father," "Prince of Peace."*

SONG:

THERE'S A SONG IN THE AIR

There's a song in the air!
There's a star in the sky!
There's a mother's deep prayer
And a baby's low cry!
And the star rains its fire while the beautiful sing,
For the manger of Bethlehem cradles a King!

There's a tumult of joy
O'er the wonderful birth,
For the virgin's sweet boy
Is the Lord of the earth.
And the star rains its fire while the beautiful sing,
For the manger of Bethlehem cradles a King!

In the light of that star
Lies redemption unfurled
And that song from afar
Has swept over the world.
Ev'ry hearth is aflame, and the beautiful sing
In the homes of the nations that Jesus is King!

We rejoice in the light
And we echo the song
That comes down thro' the night
From the heavenly throng.
And we shout to the lovely evangel they bring,
And we greet in His cradle our Savior and King!

—Josiah G. Holland and Karl P. Harrington

> *Luke 2:1-6 (page _____ in the New Testament): At that time Emperor Augustus ordered a census to be taken throughout the Roman Empire. When this first census took place, Quirinius was the governor of Syria. Everyone, then, went to register himself, each to his own hometown. Joseph went from the town of Nazareth in Galilee to the town of Bethlehem in Judea, the birthplace of King David. Joseph went there because he was a descendant of David. He went to register with Mary, who was promised in marriage to him. She was pregnant, and while they were in Bethlehem, the time came for her to have her baby.*

SONG:

O LITTLE TOWN OF BETHLEHEM

O Little town of Bethlehem, How still we see thee lie!
Above thy deep and dreamless sleep. The silent stars go by;
Yet in thy dark streets shineth The everlasting Light;
The hopes and fears of all the years Are met in thee tonight.

For Christ is born of Mary, And gathered all above,
While mortals sleep, the angels keep Their watch of wond'ring love.
O morning stars, together, Proclaim the holy birth,
And praises sing to God the King, And peace to men on earth!

How silently, how silently The wondrous gift is given!
So God imparts to human hearts The blessings of His heaven.
No ear may hear His coming, But in this world of sin,
Where meek souls will receive Him, still
The dear Christ enters in.

O holy child of Bethlehem! Descend to us, we pray;
Cast out our sin, and enter in, Be born in us today!
We hear the Christmas angels The great glad tidings tell;
O come to us, abide with us, Our Lord Immanuel!

—Phillips Brooks and Lewis H. Redner

> *Luke 2:7 (page _____ in the New Testament): She gave birth to her first son, wrapped Him in cloths and laid Him in a manger—there was no room for them to stay in the inn.*

SONG:

AWAY IN A MANGER

Away in a manger, no crib for a bed,
The little Lord Jesus laid down His sweet head;
The stars in the sky looked down where He lay,
The little Lord Jesus, asleep on the hay.

The cattle are lowing, the Baby awakes,
But little Lord Jesus, no crying He makes;
I love Thee, Lord Jesus! look down from the sky.
And stay by my cradle till morning is nigh.

Be near me, Lord Jesus, I ask Thee to stay
Close by me forever, and love me, I pray;
Bless all the dear children in Thy tender care,
And fit us for heaven to live with Thee there.

—Anonymous and James R. Murray

> *Luke 2:8-12 (page _____ in the New Testament): There were some shepherds in that part of the country who were spending the night in the fields, taking care of their flocks. An angel of the Lord appeared to them, and the glory of the Lord shone over them. They were terribly afraid, but the angel said to them, "Don't be afraid! I am here with good news for you, which will bring great joy to all the people. This very day in David's town your Savior was born—Christ the Lord! And this is what will prove it to you: you will find a baby wrapped in cloths and lying in a manger."*

SONG:

WHILE SHEPHERDS WATCHED THEIR FLOCKS

While shepherds watched their flocks by night,
All seated on the ground, The angel of the Lord came down,
And glory shone around, And glory shone around.

"Fear not!" said he; for mighty dread
Had seized their troubled mind; "Glad tidings of great joy I bring
To you and all mankind, To you and all mankind.

"To you, in David's town, this day Is born of David's line
The Saviour, who is Christ the Lord;
And this shall be the sign;
And this shall be the sign:

"The heavenly Babe you there shall find
To human view displayed, All meanly wrapped in swaddling clothes, And in
a manger laid,
And in a manger laid.

"All glory be to God on high,
And to the earth be peace:
Good will henceforth from heaven to men,
Begin and never cease,
Begin and never cease!"

—*Nahum Tate and arr. from George F. Handel*

> *Luke 2:13-14 (page _____ in the New Testament): Suddenly a great army of heaven's angels appeared with the angel, singing praises to God: "Glory to God in the highest heaven, and peace on earth to those with whom He is pleased!"*

SONG:

HARK! THE HERALD ANGELS SING

Hark! the herald angels sing, "Glory to the newborn King;
Peace on earth, and mercy mild; God and sinners reconciled."
Joyful, all ye nations, rise,
Join the triumph of the skies;
With angelic hosts proclaim, "Christ is born in Bethlehem!"
Hark! the herald angels sing, "Glory to the newborn King."

Christ, by highest heaven adored, Christ, the everlasting Lord:
Late in time, behold Him come, Offspring of a virgin's womb.
Veiled in flesh the God-head see,
Hail the incarnate Deity!

Pleased as man with men to dwell, Jesus our Immanuel.
Hark! the herald angels sing, "Glory to the newborn King."

Hail the heaven-born Prince of Peace! Hail the Sun of righteousness!
Light and life to all He brings, Risen with healing in His wings.
Mild He lays His glory by,
Born that man no more may die,
Born to raise the sons of earth, Born to give them second birth.
Hark! the herald angels sing, "Glory to the newborn King."

—Charles Wesley and Felix Mendelssohn

> *Luke 2:15-16 (page _____ in the New Testament): When the angels went away from them back into heaven, the shepherds said to one another, "Let's go to Bethlehem and see this thing that has happened, which the Lord has told us." So they hurried off and found Mary and Joseph and saw the baby lying in the manger.*

SONG:

SILENT NIGHT, HOLY NIGHT

Silent night, holy night,
All is calm, all is bright
Round yon virgin mother and Child!
Holy Infant so tender and mild,
Sleep in heavenly peace, Sleep in heavenly peace.

Silent night, holy night,
Darkness flies, all is light;
Shepherds hear the angels sing,
"Alleluia! hail the King!
Christ the Saviour is born, Christ the Saviour is born"

Silent night, holy night,
Son of God, love's pure light
Radiant beams from Thy holy face,
With the dawn of redeeming grace,
Jesus, Lord, at Thy birth, Jesus, Lord, at Thy birth.

Silent night, holy night,
Wondrous Star, lend thy light;
With the angels let us sing,
Alleluia to our King;
Christ the Saviour is born, Christ the Saviour is born.

—Joseph Mohr and Franz Gruber

> *Luke 2:17-20 (page _____ in the New Testament): When the shepherds saw Him, they told them what the angel had said about the Child. All who heard it were amazed at what the shepherds said. Mary remembered all these things and thought deeply about them. The shepherds went back, singing praises to God for all they had heard and seen; it had been just as the angel had told them.*

SONG:

JOY TO THE WORLD! THE LORD IS COME

Joy to the world! the Lord is come;
Let earth receive her King:
Let every heart prepare Him room,
And heaven and nature sing,
And heaven and nature sing,
And heaven, and heaven and nature sing.

Joy to the earth! The Savior reigns;
Let men their songs employ:
While fields and floods, rocks, hills, and plains
Repeat the sounding joy,
Repeat the sounding joy,
Repeat, repeat the sounding joy.

No more let sins and sorrows grow,
Nor thorns infest the ground;
He comes to make His blessings flow
Far as the curse is found
Far as the curse is found
Far as, far as the curse is found.

God's Plan for Christian Living

He rules the world with truth and grace,
And makes the nations prove
The glories of His righteousness,
And wonders of His love,
And wonders of His love,
And wonders, wonders of His love.

—Isaac Watts and arr. from George F. Handel

God's plan was for Jesus to be born as a baby in a human family.

God's plan is for Jesus to be born as a Saviour in my heart and in your heart. Has Jesus been born in your heart? Have you asked Jesus to live in your heart?

Ask Him to be born in your heart today.

> The true meaning of Christmas is Jesus living in your life every day!

SONG:
INTO MY HEART

Into my heart, into my heart.
Come into my heart, Lord Jesus;
Come in today; Come in to stay;
Come into my heart, Lord Jesus.

—Harry D. Clarke

DAILY BIBLE READINGS—Read from the Bible in your language and from the Good News Bible/Sunday School Bible:

Sunday	Luke 1:46-49
Monday	Luke 1:67-69
Tuesday	Luke 2:13-15
Wednesday	Luke 2:16-20
Thursday	Matthew 2:1-2
Friday	Matthew 2:9-11
Saturday	John 3:16

(Words: Used by Permission CCI #477319)

Part II: Christmas Celebration

Lesson 12

Looking Back, Looking Ahead

This is a review of Part I: The Beginning of the Christian Life, as we prepare to go into Part III: The Christian Life—A New Kind of Living!

> *Memory Verse: Matthew 16:24 (page _____ in the New Testament): Then Jesus said to His disciples, "If anyone wants to come with Me, he must forget himself, carry his cross, and follow Me."*

Answer the following questions in your own words:

1. How do you become a Christian?

   _____

   _____

   _____

2. How is your life different if you are a Christian?

   _____

   _____

   _____

3. What helps you to grow in the Christian life?

   _____

   _____

   _____

4. In the past three months, I have…

   - _____
   - _____
   - _____
   - _____

5. In the next three months, I want to…

   - _____
   - _____
   - _____
   - _____

You may have questions about some of the things you have studied. Ask your teacher to help you answer any question you have.

DAILY BIBLE READINGS—Read from the Bible in your language and from the Good News Bible/Sunday School Bible:

Sunday	Ephesians 3:14-19
Monday	Ephesians 3:20-21
Tuesday	Psalm 100
Wednesday	Colossians 2:6-7
Thursday	Philippians 3:12-14.
Friday	Colossians 1:9-14
Saturday	Romans 12:1-2

Part III:

The Christian Life—A New Kind of Living!

Part III: The Christian Life—A New Kind of Living!

Lesson 13

The Power in the Christian Life

> *Memory Verse: Acts 1:8 (page _____ in the New Testament): "When the Holy Spirit comes upon you, you will be filled with power, and you will be witnesses for Me in Jerusalem, in all of Judea and Samaria, and to the ends of the earth."*

We know God in three ways:

We know Him as God, the Father—our Creator.

We know Him as God, the Son—our Savior.

We know Him as God, the Holy Spirit—our power.

The POWER of the Christian life IS the HOLY SPIRIT.

1. **Jesus promised His Holy Spirit to everyone who believes in Him. You believe in Him when you are born again. When you are born again, the Holy Spirit comes to live in you forever.**

    John 14:16 (page _____ in the New Testament): "I will ask the Father, and He will give you another Helper, who will stay with you forever."

2. **The Holy Spirit is the power of the Christian life.**

    2 Timothy 1:7 (page _____ in the New Testament): For the Spirit that God has given us does not make us timid; instead, His Spirit fills us with power, love, and self-control.

3. **The Holy Spirit is the power to understand the Bible. Jesus was going to leave His disciples. He knew they would not know what to do without Him. He told them God would send a Helper to make them remember and understand the things He had told them. The things He told them are a part of what we now know as the Bible.**

John 14:26 (page _____ in the New Testament): "The Helper, the Holy Spirit, whom the Father will send in My name, will teach you everything and make you remember all that I have told you."

4. **The Holy Spirit is the power to grow as a Christian. When a person is born again, he is born as a spiritual baby. He needs to grow and understand more about how to live the Christian life.**

   2 Corinthians 3:18 (page _____ in the New Testament): All of us, then, reflect the glory of the Lord with uncovered faces; and that same glory, coming from the Lord, who is the Spirit, transforms us into His likeness in an ever greater degree of glory.

5. **The Holy Spirit is the power to witness. We witness when we tell about God's love. The Holy Spirit is the power to do this.**

   Acts 1:8 (page _____ in the New Testament): "But when the Holy Spirit comes upon you, you will be filled with power, and you will be witnesses for Me in Jerusalem, in all of Judea and Samaria, and to the ends of the earth."

For you to think about:

Do you know that the Holy Spirit lives in your life?

Do you know the power of the Holy Spirit in your life?

Do you want to know the power of the Holy Spirit in your life?

You can ask God to teach you the power of the Holy Spirit in your life.

DAILY BIBLE READINGS—Read from the Bible in your language and from the Good News Bible/Sunday School Bible:

Sunday	Ephesians 5:18
Monday	Ephesians 1:17
Tuesday	Ephesians 1:18-20
Wednesday	Ezekiel 36:26-27
Thursday	2 Timothy 1:7
Friday	Galatians 5:22-25
Saturday	Philippians 4:8-9

Lesson 14

The Need for God's Power in the Christian Life

> *Memory Verse: John 10:10b (page _____ in the New Testament): "I have come in order that you might have life—life in all its fullness."*

We know God in three ways:

We know Him as God, the Father—our Creator.
We know Him as God, the Son—our Savior.
We know Him as God, the Holy Spirit—our power.

The POWER of the Christian life IS the HOLY SPIRIT.

1. **God made man free to choose. A man's human nature makes him want to choose his own way. When a man chooses his own way, he is separated from God.**

   Romans 3:23 (page _____ in the New Testament): Everyone has sinned and is far away from God's saving presence.

2. **A man is a Christian when he chooses God's way.**

   John 3:36 (page _____ in the New Testament): Whoever believes in the Son has eternal life; whoever disobeys the Son will not have life, but will remain under God's punishment.

3. **A Christian has God's Holy Spirit in his life.**

   Ephesians 1:13 (page _____ in the New Testament): And you also became God's people when you heard the true message, the Good News that brought you salvation. You believed in Christ, and God put His stamp of ownership on you by giving you the Holy Spirit He had promised.

God's Plan for Christian Living

4. **A Christian still has his old human nature in his life. The old human nature and the new spiritual nature are always fighting each other in the Christian life.**

    Galatians 5:17 (page _____ in the New Testament): For what our human nature wants is opposed to what the Spirit wants, and what the Spirit wants is opposed to what our human nature wants. These two are enemies, and this means that you cannot do what you want to do.

5. **A Christian is a Christian forever. A Christian is always God's child.**

    John 10:27-28 (page _____ in the New Testament): "My sheep listen to My voice; I know them, and they follow Me. I give them eternal life, and they shall never die. No one can snatch them away from me."

    When you were born physically, you could not be "unborn" physically. When you are born spiritually, you cannot be "unborn" spiritually.

    Answer the following questions in your own words:

1. What separates you from God?
    _____

2. Who lives in a Christian's life?
    _____

3. What makes living the Christian life difficult?
    _____

4. How long will you be God's child?
    _____

DAILY BIBLE READINGS—Read from the Bible in your language and from the Good News Bible/Sunday School Bible:

Sunday	Romans 8:35-39
Monday	Romans 8:5-6
Tuesday	Romans 8:7-8
Wednesday	Romans 8:9-11
Thursday	Romans 8:12-13
Friday	Romans 8:14-15
Saturday	Romans 8:16-17

Part III: The Christian Life—A New Kind of Living!

Lesson 15

Choosing the Fullness of God's Power

> *Memory Verse: John 10:10b (page _____ in the New Testament): "I have come in order that you might have life—life in all its fullness."*

The Holy Spirit lives in all Christians, but all Christians are not filled with the Holy Spirit. Christians have life in all its fullness when they choose to be filled with God's Spirit.

1. **You can be filled with the Holy Spirit when you . . .**

    i. Truly want God to control your life and to give you the power He promised.

    Matthew 5:6 (page _____ in the New Testament): "Happy are those whose greatest desire is to do what God requires; God will satisfy them fully!"

    ii. Confess your sins. God forgave all your sins when you chose His way. Sometimes you still choose your way. Choosing your way is sin. Sin separates you from God. When you confess your sins to God, He takes them away. Then you are clean and ready to be filled with the Holy Spirit.

    1 John 1:9 (page _____ in the New Testament): But if we confess our sins to God, He will keep His promise and do what is right: He will forgive us our sins and purify us from all our wrongdoing.

    iii. Offer every part of your life to God. Give God complete control of your life.

    Romans 12:1-2 (page _____ in the New Testament): So then, my brothers, because of God's great mercy to us I appeal to you: Offer yourselves as a living sacrifice to God, dedicated to His service and pleasing to Him. This is the true worship that you should offer. Do not conform yourselves to the standards of this world, but let God transform you inwardly by a complete change of your mind. Then you will be able to know the will of God—what is good and is pleasing to Him and is perfect.

God's Plan for Christian Living

    iv. Accept the filling of the Holy Spirit by faith because . . .

    The Bible commands it. Ephesians 5:18b (page ____ in the New Testament): Be filled with the Spirit.

    The Bible promises it. Luke 11:13 (page ____ in the New Testament): "As bad as you are, you know how to give good things to your children. How much more, then, will the Father in heaven give the Holy Spirit to those who ask Him."

2. **You can know you are filled with the Holy Spirit.**

   If you asked God to fill you with His Holy Spirit, you know He did because He does what He promises. Some people have special feelings when they are filled with the Holy Spirit. Some people do not. Do not trust your feelings. Trust in God and His Word.

   1 John 5:14-15 (page ____ in the New Testament): We have courage in God's presence, because we are sure that He hears us if we ask Him for anything that is according to His will. He hears us whenever we ask Him; and since we know that is true, we know also that He gives us what we ask from Him.

Have you asked God to fill you with His Holy Spirit?

> *If you have not, you can ask God to fill you with His Holy Spirit right now.*
>
> *If you have asked God to fill you with His Holy Spirit, write your:*
>
> Name: _____
>
>   Date: _____

DAILY BIBLE READINGS—Read from the Bible in your language and from the Good News Bible/Sunday School Bible:

Sunday	Acts 2:38-39
Monday	John 14:15-17
Tuesday	John 14:1-21
Wednesday	John 14:22-24
Thursday	John 14:25-26
Friday	John 14:27
Saturday	John 14:28-31

Part III: The Christian Life—A New Kind of Living!

Lesson 16

The Result of God's Power in the Christian Life

Memory Verse: Galatians 5:25 (page _____ in the New Testament): The Spirit has given us life; He must also control our lives.

Your life is changed when you . . .

- choose God's way for your life.
- offer every part of your life to God.
- accept God's power in your life by faith.

1. **Everything good is a gift from God. God gives many good gifts. You must receive God's gifts in your life for them to be yours.**

    James 1:17 (page _____ in the New Testament): Every good gift and every perfect present comes from heaven; it comes down from God, the Creator of the heavenly lights, who does not change or cause darkness by turning.

2. **God's Spirit produces in your life . . .**

    Galatians 5:22b-23 (page _____ in the New Testament): . . . love, joy, peace, patience, kindness, goodness, faithfulness, humility, and self-control.

3. **Your life will show other people the result of God's power in your life.**

    Zacchaeus did bad things. He took money that was not his. One day he chose God's way for his life. He believed in Jesus. His life was changed. Other people could see the result of God's power in his life. He gave back the money he had taken and he helped the poor.

    Luke 19:8 (page _____ in the New Testament): Zacchaeus stood up and said to the Lord, "Listen, Sir! I will give half by belongings to the poor, and if I have cheated anyone, I will pay him back four times as much."

    Read Luke 19:1-10 (page _____ in the New Testament).

God's Plan for Christian Living

How do you accept God's power in your LIFE?

_____

Have YOU accepted God's power in your life?

_____

God's power in your life changes the way you live. Can you see a change in your life?

_____

4. **Discouragement: an attack of Satan.**

   Job 7:14-16 (page _____ in the Old Testament): But you—you terrify me with dreams; you send me visions and nightmares until I would rather be strangled than live in this miserable body. I give up; I am tired of living. Leave me alone. My life makes no sense.

   > *Psalm 56:9b-11 (page _____ in the Old Testament): I know this: God is on my side—the LORD, whose promises I praise. In Him I trust, and I will not be afraid. What can a mere human being do to me?*

   1. Do you KNOW that God loves you ALL the time?   Yes _____ No _____

   2. Do you know someone that you need to love the way God loves you? Write his/her name here: _____

DAILY BIBLE READINGS—Read from the Bible in your language and from the Good News Bible/Sunday School Bible:

Sunday	Psalm 65:9b-11
Monday	1 John 3:16; 1 John 3:1a
Tuesday	Romans 5:8
Wednesday	Psalm 51:3-4
Thursday	Psalm 56:2
Friday	Psalm 22:14-15
Saturday	Job 7:14-15

Part III: The Christian Life—A New Kind of Living!

Lesson 17

God Loves You

Memory Verse: John 3:16 (page ____ in the New Testament): For God loved the world so much that He gave His only Son, so that everyone who believes in Him may not die, but have eternal life.

Love is wanting the best for another person even if it is a cost to yourself.

1. **God loves (wants the best for) everyone in the world.**

    John 3:16 (page ____ in the New Testament): For God loved the world so much that He gave His only Son, so that everyone who believes in Him may not die, but have eternal life.

2. **God loves you (wants the best for you) enough to die for you.**

    1 John 3:16a (page ____ in the New Testament): This is how we know what love is: Christ gave His life for us.

3. **God loves you (wants the best for you) even when you do not love Him.**

    Romans 5:8 (page ____ in the New Testament): But God has shown us how much He loves us—it was while we were still sinners that Christ died for us!

4. **God loves you (wants the best for you) even when you do not love yourself.**

    1 John 3:1 (page ____ in the New Testament): See how much the Father has loved us! His love is so great that we are called God's children—and so, in fact, we are.

5. **Things that can make you not love yourself:**

    i. Your sins—guilt.

    Psalm 51:3-4 (page ____ in the Old Testament): I recognize my faults; I am always conscious of my sins. I have sinned against you—only against you—and done what You consider evil. So You are right in judging me; You are justified in condemning me.

ii. Criticism from other people.

Psalm 56:2 (page ____ in the Old Testament): All day long my opponents attack me. There are so many who fight against me.

iii. The way you feel.

Psalm 22:14-15 (page ____ in the Old Testament): My strength is gone, gone like water spilled on the ground. All my bones are out of joint; my heart is like melted wax. My throat is as dry as dust, and my tongue sticks to the roof of my mouth. You have left me for dead in the dust.

iv. Discouragement—an attack of Satan.

Job 7:14-16 (page ____ in the Old Testament): But you—you terrify me with dreams; you send me visions and nightmares until I would rather be strangled than live in this miserable body. I give up; I am tired of living. Leave me alone. My life makes no sense.

> *Psalm 56:9b-11 (page ____ in the Old Testament): . . . I know this: God is on my side—the Lord, whose promises I praise. In Him I trust, and I will not be afraid. What can a mere human being do to me?*

1. Do you KNOW that God loves you ALL the time?   Yes_____ No_____

2. Do you know someone that you need to love the way God loves you? Write his/her name here: _____

DAILY BIBLE READINGS—Read from the Bible in your language and from the Good News Bible/Sunday School Bible:

Sunday	Psalm 56:9b-11
Monday	1 John 3:16; 1 John 3:1a
Tuesday	Romans 5:8
Wednesday	Psalm 51:3-4
Thursday	Psalm 56:2
Friday	Psalm 22:14-15
Saturday	Job 7:14-15

Part III: The Christian Life—A New Kind of Living!

Lesson 18

God Loves You (Continued)

Memory Verse: James 1:17 (page _____ in the New Testament): Every good gift and every perfect present comes from heaven; it comes down from God, the Creator of the heavenly lights, who does not change or cause darkness by turning.

Christians receive special gifts because of God's love.

1. **God gives you eternal life.**

   When you are born physically, you cannot be "unborn" physically. When you are born spiritually, you cannot be "unborn" spiritually. When you are born spiritually, God gives you eternal life. Eternal life is life with God forever—without end!

   John 10:28 (page _____ in the New Testament): "I give them eternal life, and they shall never die. No one can snatch them away from Me."

2. **God gives you every good gift and every perfect present. Some of the good gifts and perfect presents are . . .**

   - God's kind of love
   - God's presence
   - God's peace

   James 1:17 (page _____ in the New Testament): Every good gift and every perfect present comes from heaven; it comes down from God, the Creator of the heavenly lights, who does not change or cause darkness by turning.

God's Plan for Christian Living

3. **God gives you complete forgiveness.**

   Jesus Christ died on the cross to forgive all the sins of all the world. You receive God's forgiveness for your sins when you choose God's way for your life. After you choose God's way for your life . . .

   i. You will never be separated ETERNALLY from God because of your sins.

      Micah 7:19 (page _____ in the Old Testament): You will be merciful to us once again. You will trample our sins underfoot and send them to the bottom of the sea!

      Psalm 103:12 (page _____ in the Old Testament): As far as the east is from the west, so far does He remove our sins from us.

      Jeremiah 31:34b (page _____ in the Old Testament): "I will forgive their sins and I will no longer remember their wrongs. I, the LORD, have spoken."

   ii. You WILL be separated from KNOWING God's presence in your life because of your sins. To know God's presence in your life, you must obey God:

   Confess your sins to God.

   Ask God to forgive you. Thank God for His forgiveness.

   Ask the person that you hurt to forgive you.

   Make things right with the person whom you hurt.

   1 John 1:9 (page _____ in the New Testament): But if we confess our sins to God, He will keep His promise and do what is right: He will forgive us our sins and purify us from all our wrongdoing.

   Matthew 5:23-24 (page _____ in the New Testament): So if you are about to offer your gift to God at the altar and there you remember that your brother has something against you, leave your gift there in front of the altar, go at once and make peace with your brother, and then come back and offer your gift to God.

Answer the following questions:

1. Do you know that your life with God will never end?   Yes _____ No _____

2. Do you know that God has good gifts for you?   Yes _____ No _____

3. Do you know that God gives you complete forgiveness?   Yes _____ No _____

Part III: The Christian Life—A New Kind of Living!

4. Do you need to make things right with someone?   Yes _____ No _____

5. If your answer to the last question was "yes," will you make things right with that person?   Yes _____ No _____

DAILY BIBLE READINGS—Read from the Bible in your language and from the Good News Bible/Sunday School Bible:

Sunday	James 1:17
Monday	John 10:28
Tuesday	Micah 7:19
Wednesday	Psalm 103:12
Thursday	Jeremiah 31:24
Friday	John 1:9
Saturday	Matthew 5:23-24

God's Plan for Christian Living

Lesson 19

God Tells You

> *God Tells You Memory Verse: John 15:12 (page _____ in the New Testament): "My commandment is this: love one another, just as I love you."*

God tells you to love Him and to love people. God tells you to love Him and to love people the way He loves you. God's love wants the best for you. God loves you so much He came to earth in a human body. God loves you so much He lived and died and rose again for you.

1. **God tells you to love Him.**

    Matthew 22:37 (page _____ in the New Testament): Jesus answered, "Love the Lord your God with all your heart, with all your soul, and with all your mind."

2. **God tells you to love people.**

    Matthew 22:39b (page _____ in the New Testament): Jesus said, . . . "Love your neighbor as you love yourself."

3. **God tells you to love your family. God made the family. God loves the family. God wants the members of the family to love each other.**

    Genesis 2:18 (page _____ in the Old Testament): Then the LORD God said, "It is not good for the man to live alone. I will make a suitable companion to help him."

4. **God tells you to accept people.**

    You can love and accept people without loving and accepting what they do. Jesus told a story about a father who loved and accepted his son. The father did not love or accept what his son did.

    Read Luke 15:11-24 (page _____ in the New Testament).

Part III: The Christian Life—A New Kind of Living!

    i. The son asked the father for his share of the family property. The son left home. The son spent all of his money for bad things (Luke 15:11-16).

    ii. The son decided to go home (Luke 15:17-20a).

    iii. The father accepted his son just the way he was. The father loved his son (Luke 15:20b-24).

5. Loving is accepting another person. You can love and accept another person by remembering...

    i. God made the person in God's image just as He made you.

Genesis 1:27 (page _____ in the Old Testament): So God created human beings, making them to be like Himself. He created them male and female.

    ii. God loves the person just as He loves you.

John 3:16 (page _____ in the New Testament): For God loved the world so much that He gave His only Son, so that everyone who believes in Him may not die but have eternal life.

    iii. Jesus died for the person just as He died for you.

John 3:16 (page _____ in the New Testament): For God loved the world so much that He gave His only Son, so that everyone who believes in Him may not die but have eternal life.

Some lessons that help you love and accept another person are...

1. _____

2. _____

3. _____

4. _____

DAILY BIBLE READINGS—Read from the Bible in your language and from the Good News Bible/Sunday School Bible:

Sunday	John 15:12-17
Monday	Matthew 22:37-40
Tuesday	Genesis 2:18
Wednesday	Luke 15:11-14
Thursday	Luke 15:15-19
Friday	Luke 15:20-24
Saturday	John 15:12

Lesson 20

God Tells You (Continued)

Memory Verse: John 15:12 (page _____ in the New Testament): "My commandment is this: love one another, just as I love you."

> God tells you to love Him.
>
> God tells you to love people.
>
> God tells you to love your family.
>
> Loving is accepting people.
>
> Loving is forgiving people.

1. **One day Jesus was teaching in the temple. Some Jewish leaders brought a woman to Him. The woman had been caught in the act of adultery. Jesus forgave the woman her sins.**

   Read John 8:1-11 (page _____ in the New Testament).
   i. The woman had done a very bad thing. She had sinned. She had committed adultery (John 8:1-3).
   ii. Jewish law commanded that she be killed (John 8:4-5).
   iii. Jesus made the Jewish leaders understand that they were sinners also (John 8:7-9).
   iv. Jesus did not command that the woman be killed. Jesus forgave the woman's sins. Jesus told the woman to change her way of living (John 8:10-11).

2. **Loving is forgiving another person. You can forgive another person . . .**
   i. By remembering you are a sinner too.

      Romans 3:23 (page _____ in the New Testament): Everyone has sinned and is far away from God's saving presence.

Part III: The Christian Life—A New Kind of Living!

    ii. With God's help.

    1 John 5:14-15 (page _____ in the New Testament): We have courage in God's presence because we are sure He hears us if we ask Him for anything that is according to His will. He hears us whenever we ask Him; and since we know this is true, we know also that He gives us what we ask from Him.

    iii. As God forgives you.

    Psalm 103:12 (page _____ in the Old Testament): As far as the east is from the west, so far does He remove our sins from us.

    iv. By not reminding the person of what he did.

    Micah 7:19 (page _____ in the Old Testament): You will be merciful to us once again. You will trample our sins underfoot and send them to the bottom of the sea!

    v. By not thinking about the bad thing the person did.

    Philippians 4:8 (page _____ in the New Testament): In conclusion, my brothers, fill your minds with those things that are good and that deserve praise: things that are true, noble, right, pure, lovely, and honorable.

Some lessons that help you forgive another person are . . .

1. _____

2. _____

3. _____

4. _____

DAILY BIBLE READINGS—Read from the Bible in your language and from the Good News Bible/Sunday School Bible:

Sunday	John 3:16
Monday	Romans 3:23
Tuesday	1 John 5:14-15
Wednesday	Psalm 103:12
Thursday	Micah 7:19
Friday	Philippians 4:8
Saturday	John 15:12

Lesson 21

God Tells You (Continued)

Memory Verse: John 15:12 (page _____ in the New Testament): "My commandment is this: love one another, just as I love you."

> God tells you to love Him.
>
> God tells you to love people.
>
> God tells you to love your family.
>
> Loving is accepting people.
>
> Loving is forgiving people.
>
> Loving is helping people.

1. **One day Jesus told a story about helping people. A Jewish man was on his way to Jericho. He was beaten by robbers. A Samaritan man stopped to help him. Helping is loving.**

    Read Luke 10:30-37 (page _____ in the New Testament).

    i. A Jewish man was on a trip from Jerusalem to Jericho. Some robbers beat him. They left him to die (Luke 10:30).

    ii. Two Jewish leaders passed by him. They did not stop to help him (Luke 10:31-32).

    iii. A Samaritan who came by stopped to help him (Luke 10:33).

    iv. The Samaritan took care of the man's wounds (Luke 10:34a).

    v. The Samaritan carried the man to an inn to recover from his wounds (Luke 10:34b-35).

2. **Loving is helping another person. Loving is helping another person without wanting something in return. You can help another person . . .**

i. By being kind to the person.

   Ephesians 4:32 (page _____ in the New Testament): Instead, be kind and tender-hearted to one another, and forgive one another as God has forgiven you through Christ.

ii. By treating the person as you would like for him to treat you.

   Luke 6:31 (page _____ in the New Testament—NASB): And just as you want men to treat you, treat them in the same way.

You are kind to another person when you . . .

1. _____

2. _____

3. _____

4. _____

How do you want to be treated?

1. _____

2. _____

3. _____

4. _____

DAILY BIBLE READINGS—Read from the Bible in your language and from the Good News Bible/Sunday School Bible:

Sunday	Luke 10:30
Monday	Luke 10:31-32
Tuesday	Luke 10:33
Wednesday	Luke 10:34a
Thursday	Luke 10:34b-35
Friday	Ephesians 4:32
Saturday	Luke 6:31

God's Plan for Christian Living

Lesson 22

God Tells You (Continued)

Memory Verse: John 15:12 (page _____ in the New Testament): "My commandment is this: love one another, just as I love you."

> God tells you to love Him.
>
> God tells you to love people.
>
> God tells you to love your family.
>
> Loving is accepting people.
>
> Loving is forgiving people.
>
> Loving is helping people.

Read again the story of the Good Samaritan in Luke 10:30-37 (page _____ in the New Testament).

Loving is helping another person:

1. **By being kind to the person.**

    Ephesians 4:32 (page _____ in the New Testament): Instead, be kind and tender-hearted to one another, and forgive one another as God has forgiven you.

2. **By treating the person as you would like for him to treat you.**

    Luke 6:31 (page _____ in the New Testament—NASB): "And just as you want men to treat you, treat them in the same way."

Part III: The Christian Life—A New Kind of Living!

3. **By meeting his needs.**

   i. Sometimes a person needs food. Sometimes a person needs clothes. Sometimes a person needs money.

   James 2:15-16 (page _____ in the New Testament): Suppose there are brothers or sisters who need clothes and don't have enough to eat. What good is there in your saying to them, "God bless you. Keep warm and eat well!"—if you don't give them the necessities of life?

   ii. Sometimes a person needs a friend. A friend listens to you. A friend laughs with you. A friend cries with you. A friend encourages you.

   Proverbs 17:17 (page _____ in the Old Testament): Friends always show their love. What are brothers for if not to share trouble?

   iii. A person always needs to know God loves Him.

   Romans 5:8 (page _____ in the New Testament): But God has shown us how much He loves us—it was while we were still sinners that Christ died for us!

You can help another person by . . .

1. _____

2. _____

3. _____

4. _____

DAILY BIBLE READINGS—Read from the Bible in your language and from the Good News Bible/Sunday School Bible:

Sunday	Ephesians 4:32
Monday	Luke 6:31
Tuesday	James 2:15-16
Wednesday	Proverbs 17:17
Thursday	Romans 5:8
Friday	1 John 3:18
Saturday	Proverbs 19:17

Lesson 23

God Tells You (Continued)

Memory Verse: John 15:12 (page _____ in the New Testament): "My commandment is this: love one another, just as I love you."

> God tells you to love Him.
>
> God tells you to love people.
>
> God tells you to love your family.
>
> Loving is accepting people.
>
> Loving is forgiving people.
>
> Loving is helping people.
>
> Loving is telling people God loves them.

4. **One day Jesus met a man who was sick.**

   Jesus healed the man. The man wanted to go with Jesus. Jesus said, "Go back home and tell what God has done for you."

   The man chose to obey Jesus. The man told his family and friends what Jesus had done for him.

   Read Luke 8:26-39 (page _____ in the New Testament).

5. **Loving is telling another person about God's love. You can tell about God's love by . . .**

   iv. Telling another person what the Bible says about God's love.

   God loves everyone in the world. John 3:16 (page _____ in the New Testament): For God loved the world so much that He gave His only Son, so that everyone who believes in Him may not die but have eternal life.

   God loves you enough to die for you. 1 John 3:16a (page _____ in the New Testament): This is how we know what love is: Christ gave His life for us.

Part III: The Christian Life—A New Kind of Living!

God loves you even when you do not love Him. Romans 5:8 (page ____ in the New Testament): But God has shown us how much He loves us—it was while we were still sinners that Christ died for us!

v. Telling another person he can know God's love when he chooses God's way for his life. He chooses God's way for his life when…

He believes in God and believes that Jesus is God's Son. John 3:16 (page ____ in the New Testament): For God loved the world so much that He gave His only Son, so that everyone who believes in Him may not die but have eternal life.

He asks Jesus to come into his life and obeys Him. Matthew 7:7a (page ____ in the New Testament): "Ask, and you will receive."

vi. Telling another person what God has done in your own life. You can tell how you chose God's way for your life. You can tell how your life has been changed.

Luke 8:39 (page ____ in the New Testament): "Go back home and tell what God has done for you." The man went through the town, telling what Jesus had done for him.

Answer the following questions in your own words:
---

1. Can you tell how you chose God's way for your life?
   _____

2. Will you tell someone how you chose God's way for your life?
   _____

3. How has Jesus changed your life?
   _____

DAILY BIBLE READINGS—Read from the Bible in your language and from the Good News Bible/Sunday School Bible:

Sunday	Luke 8:26-27
Monday	Luke 8:28-29
Tuesday	Luke 8:30-31
Wednesday	Luke 8:32-33
Thursday	Luke 8:34-35
Friday	Luke 8:36-37
Saturday	Luke 8:38-39

Lesson 24

God Tells You (Continued)

Memory Verse: John 15:12 (page ____ in the New Testament): "My commandment is this: love one another, just as I love you."

> God tells you to love Him.
>
> God tells you to love people.
>
> God tells you to love your family.
>
> Loving is accepting people.
>
> Loving is forgiving people.
>
> Loving is helping people.
>
> Loving is telling people God loves them.
>
> Loving is supporting missionaries who tell people God loves them.

God had a plan to love people.

God had a plan to tell people about His love.

Matthew 28:18-20 (page ____ in the New Testament): Jesus drew near and said to them, "I have been given all authority in heaven and on earth. Go then, to all peoples everywhere and make them My disciples: baptize them in the name of the Father, the Son, and the Holy Spirit, and teach them to obey everything I have commanded you. And I will be with you always, to the end of the age.

Part III: The Christian Life—A New Kind of Living!

A person who tells people about God's love through Jesus is a Christian. A person whose life's work is going to places near or far telling people about God's love through Jesus is a Christian missionary. These people are obeying Jesus' command to go to "Jerusalem, Judea, Samaria, and the ends of the earth" to tell about God's love. Christian missionaries are supported by people who give money to help them.

Acts 1:8 (page ____ in the New Testament): "But when the Holy Spirit comes upon you, you will be filled with power, and you will be witnesses for Me in Jerusalem, in all of Judea and Samaria, and to the ends of the earth."

Missionaries tell people about God's love in many ways. Some missionaries are . . .

preachers	agriculture workers
health workers	church planters
teachers	chaplains
musicians	mission center directors
radio and TV workers	student workers
publishers	homemakers
business administrators	dormitory parents

You can be a part of God's plan to tell people about His love. You are a part of God's plan to tell people about His love when you pray for missionaries. You are a part of God's plan to tell people about His love when you give money to support missionaries.

Discuss with your teacher the ways your church supports missionaries in your hometown, your state, the United States, and around the world.

DAILY BIBLE READINGS—Read from the Bible in your language and from the Good News Bible/Sunday School Bible:

Sunday	Matthew 28:18-20
Monday	Mark 16:15
Tuesday	Luke 24:47
Wednesday	John 20:21
Thursday	Acts 1:8
Friday	Luke 10:2
Saturday	Romans 10:14-15

Lesson 25

God Tells You (Continued)

Memory Verse: John 15:12 (page _____ in the New Testament): "My commandment is this: love one another, just as I love you."

> God tells you to love Him.
>
> God tells you to love people.
>
> God tells you to love your family.
>
> Loving is accepting people.
>
> Loving is forgiving people.
>
> Loving is helping people.
>
> Loving is telling people God loves them.
>
> Loving is supporting missionaries who tell people God loves them.

Discuss with your teacher the following questions to understand who supports missionaries:

>> where the money comes from
>> how the money is distributed
>> how you can be a part of praying and giving

Part III: The Christian Life—A New Kind of Living!

1. What denomination, church, or para-church group are you a part of?
   _____

2. Where is your church located?
   _____

3. What kind of missions programs does it support?
   - North American Missions: All 50 states and protectorates? Canada?
     _____
   - Global Missions: What countries?
     _____
   - Short-Term Missions: What countries?
     _____

4. Who leads these various mission programs/departments?
   _____

5. How are missionaries selected?
   _____

6. How are missionaries trained?
   _____

7. Approximately how many people are involved, both paid staff and volunteers?
   _____

8. Who funds the salaries, travel, resources, supplies, equipment, etc.?
   _____

9. Is a percentage of your church's/organization's budget designated for missions?
   _____

10. Are there specific offerings, plus designated funds in your church's budget, to provide additional funds for these expenses?
    _____

God uses people in many different ways to tell others about His love. God can use you to tell others about His love.

DAILY BIBLE READINGS—Read from the Bible in your language and from the Good News Bible/Sunday School Bible:

Sunday	Mark 16:15
Monday	Luke 24:47
Tuesday	John 20:21
Wednesday	Romans 10:15
Thursday	Acts 26:18
Friday	Luke 10:2
Saturday	Matthew 28:18-20

Part IV:

Easter Celebration—God's Plan Fulfilled

God had a plan.

*God loved people and He wanted people to love Him.
God sent His Son to earth to live among people.
Jesus told people about God.
God's plan was for His Son to come to earth
and die for the sin of the world.*

1 Peter 1:19-21 (page _____ in the New Testament): It was the costly sacrifice of Christ, who was like a lamb without defect or flaw. He had been chosen by God before the creation of the world and was revealed in these last days for your sake. Through Him you believe in God, who raised Him from death and gave Him glory; and so your faith and hope are fixed on God.

Part IV: Easter Celebration—God's Plan Fulfilled

Lesson 26

Jesus' Special Supper with His Friends

Memory Verse: Philippians 2:7-8 (page _____ in the New Testament): Instead of this, of His own free will He gave up all He had, and took the nature of a servant. He became like man and appeared in human likeness. He was humble and walked the path of obedience all the way to death—His death on the cross.

God showed His love for His friends in a special way. God's friends are those who choose His way, who love Him and obey Him. God's friends are called CHRISTIANS.

1. **Jesus was with His friends the night before He died.**

    John 13:1 (page _____ in the New Testament): It was now the day before the Passover Festival. Jesus knew that the hour had come for Him to leave this world and go to the Father. He had always loved those in the world who were His own, and He loved them to the very end.

2. **Jesus and His friends ate the Passover Supper together.**

    John 13:2 (page _____ in the New Testament): Jesus and His disciples were at supper. The Devil had already put into the heart of Judas, the son of Simon Iscariot, the thought of betraying Jesus.

3. **Jesus washed the feet of His friends.**

    John 13:3-5 (page _____ in the New Testament): Jesus knew that the Father had given Him complete power; He knew that He had come from God and was going to God. So He rose from the table, took off His outer garment, and tied a towel around His waist. Then He poured some water into a washbasin and began to wash the disciples' feet and dry them with the towel around His waist.

91

God's Plan for Christian Living

　　i.　Jesus showed how He loved His friends.

　　ii.　Jesus showed how He wants His friends to love one another:

Philippians 2:6-8 (page _____ in the New Testament): He always had the nature of God, but He did not think that by force He should try to become equal with God. Instead of this, of His own free will He gave up all He had, and took the nature of a servant. He became like man and appeared in human likeness. He was humble and walked the path of obedience all the way to death—His death on the cross.

4.　**Jesus gave new meaning to the Passover Supper. Jesus gave a new way to observe the Passover Supper. Christians call this observance the LORD'S SUPPER.**

　　i.　The bread that Jesus broke and gave His friends was a picture of His death.

Matthew 26:26 (page _____ in the New Testament): While they were eating, Jesus took a piece of bread, gave a prayer of thanks, broke it, and gave it to His disciples. "Take and eat it," He said; "this is My body."

　　ii.　The wine in the cup that Jesus gave His friends was a picture of His blood that He shed on the cross.

Matthew 26:27-28 (page _____ in the New Testament): Then He took a cup, gave thanks to God, and gave it to them. "Drink it, all of you," He said; "this is My blood, which seals God's covenant, My blood poured out for many for the forgiveness of sins."

5.　**The LORD'S SUPPER is for Christians today.**

1 Corinthians 11:23-26 (page _____ in the New Testament): For I received from the Lord the teaching that I passed on to you: that the Lord Jesus, on the night He was betrayed, took a piece of bread, gave thanks to God, broke it, and said, "This is My body, which is for you. Do this in memory of Me." In the same way, after the supper, He took the cup and said, "This cup is God's new covenant, sealed with My blood. Whenever you drink it, do so in memory of Me." This means that every time you eat this bread and drink from this cup you proclaim the Lord's death until He comes.

> Answer the following questions in your own words:

1.　What does the Lord's Supper mean?

_____

2. Who participates in the Lord's Supper?

   _____

3. Have you participated in the Lord's Supper?

   _____

4. What did it mean to you?

   _____

DAILY BIBLE READINGS—Read from the Bible in your language and from the Good News Bible/Sunday School Bible:

Sunday	John 13:1
Monday	John 13:2
Tuesday	John 13:3-5
Wednesday	Philippians 2:6-8
Thursday	Matthew 26:26
Friday	Matthew 26:27-28
Saturday	1 Corinthians 11:23-26

Lesson 27

Jesus in the Garden of Gethsemane

> *Memory Verse: Luke 22:42 (page ____ in the New Testament):* "Father," He said, "if You will, take this cup of suffering away from Me. Not My will, however, but Your will be done."

When Jesus and His friends had finished the Lord's Supper, they went to the Mount of Olives.

Matthew 26:30 (page ____ in the New Testament): Then they sang a hymn and went out to the Mount of Olives.

1. **Jesus and His friends went to the Garden of Gethsemane on the Mount of Olives.**

   Luke 22:39 (page ____ in the New Testament): Jesus left the city and went, as He usually did, to the Mount of Olives; and the disciples went with Him.

2. **Jesus went to pray alone.**

   Luke 22:41 (page ____ in the New Testament): Then He went off from them about the distance of a stone's throw and knelt down and prayed.

3. **Jesus prayed that He would not have to die.**

   Luke 22:42a (page ____ in the New Testament): "Father," He said, "if You will, take this cup of suffering away from Me."

4. **Jesus was willing to choose God's way.**

   Luke 22:42b (page ____ in the New Testament): "Not My will, however, but Your will be done."

Part IV: Easter Celebration—God's Plan Fulfilled

5. **An angel came to strengthen/help Jesus when He was crushed with sorrow.**

    Luke 22:43-44 (page _____ in the New Testament): An angel from heaven appeared to Him and strengthened Him. In great anguish He prayed even more fervently; His sweat was like drops of blood falling to the ground.

6. **His friends were tired and went to sleep.**

    Luke 22:45 (page _____ in the New Testament): Rising from His prayer, He went back to the disciples and found them asleep, worn out by their grief.

7. **Jesus was betrayed by His friend Judas.**

    Luke 22:47-48 (page _____ in the New Testament): Jesus was still speaking when a crowd arrived, led by Judas, one of the twelve disciples. He came up to Jesus to kiss Him. But Jesus said, "Judas, is it with a kiss that you betray the Son of Man?"

8. **The friends of Jesus wanted to fight to save His life.**

    Luke 22:49-53 (page _____ in the New Testament): When the disciples who were with Jesus saw what was going to happen, they asked, "Shall we use our swords, Lord?" And one of them struck the High Priest's slave and cut off his right ear. But Jesus said, "Enough of this!" He touched the man's ear and healed him. Then Jesus said to the chief priests and the officers of the Temple guard and the elders who had come there to get Him, "Did you have to come with swords and clubs, as though I were an outlaw? I was with you in the Temple every day, and you did not try to arrest Me. But this is your hour to act, when the power of darkness rules."

Jesus CHOSE God's way. He CHOSE to die on the cross for OUR sins.

Philippians 2:8 (page _____ in the New Testament): He was humble and walked the path of obedience all the way to death—His death on the cross.

John 3:16 (page _____ in the New Testament): For God loved the world so much that He gave His only Son, so that everyone who believes in Him may not die but have eternal life.

Do you know how important it is to pray alone? Jesus did.

Do you have a special time to pray?

Why was Jesus willing to die on the cross?

DAILY BIBLE READINGS—Read from the Bible in your language and from the Good News Bible/Sunday School Bible:

Sunday	Matthew 26:26-30
Monday	Luke 22:39-40
Tuesday	Luke 22:41-42
Wednesday	Luke 22:43-44
Thursday	Luke 22:45-48
Friday	Luke 22:49-53
Saturday	Philippians 2:8; John 3:16

Part IV: Easter Celebration—God's Plan Fulfilled

Lesson 28

Jesus' Trial

Memory Verse: Mark 14:61b-62a (page _____ in the New Testament): Again the High Priest questioned Him, "Are You the Messiah, the Son of the Blessed God?" "I am," answered Jesus, . . .

1. **Jesus was arrested by the soldiers and taken to the house of the High Priest.**

    Luke 22:54 (page _____ in the New Testament): They arrested Jesus and took Him away into the house of the High Priest; and Peter followed at a distance.

2. **Peter denied knowing Jesus.**

    Luke 22:55-57 (page _____ in the New Testament): A fire had been lit in the center of the courtyard, and Peter joined those who were sitting around it. When one of the servant girls saw him sitting there at the fire, she looked straight at him and said, "This man too was with Jesus!" But Peter denied it, "Woman, I don't even know Him!"

3. **Peter denied knowing Jesus a second time.**

    Luke 22:58 (page _____ in the New Testament): After a little while a man noticed Peter and said, "You are one of them, too!" But Peter answered, "Man, I am not!"

4. **Peter denied knowing Jesus a third time.**

    Luke 22:59-60 (page _____ in the New Testament): And about an hour later another man insisted strongly, "There isn't any doubt that this man was with Jesus because he also is a Galilean!" But Peter answered, "Man, I don't know what you are talking about." At once, while he was still speaking, a rooster crowed.

5. **Peter was sorry that He had denied Jesus. He repented.**

    Luke 22:61-62 (page _____ in the New Testament): The Lord turned around and looked straight at Peter, and Peter remembered that the Lord had said to him, "Before the rooster crows tonight, you will say three times that you do not know Me." Peter went out and wept bitterly.

God's Plan for Christian Living

6. **Jesus was mocked and beaten by His guards.**

    Luke 22:63-65 (page _____ in the New Testament): The men who were guarding Jesus made fun of Him and beat Him. They blindfolded Him and asked Him, "Who hit You? Guess!" And they said many other insulting things to Him.

7. **Jesus was questioned by the Jewish religious leaders.**

    i. People told lies about Jesus.

    ii. Jesus did not answer anyone.

    Mark 14:55-61a (page _____ in the New Testament): The chief priests and the whole Council tried to find some evidence against Jesus in order to put Him to death, but they could not find any. Many witnesses told lies against Jesus, but their stories did not agree. Then some men stood up and told this lie against Jesus: "We heard Him say, 'I will tear down this Temple which men have made and after three days I will build one that is not made by men.'" Not even they, however, could make their stories agree. The High Priest stood up in front of them all and questioned Jesus, "Have You no answer to the accusation they bring against You?" But Jesus kept quiet and would not say a word.

8. **The High Priest asked Jesus, "Are You the Messiah?"**

    Mark 14:61b (page _____ in the New Testament): Again the High Priest questioned Him, "Are You the Messiah, the Son of the Blessed God?"

9. **Jesus answered the High Priest, "I AM!"**

    Mark 14:62 (page _____ in the New Testament): "I am," answered Jesus, "and you will all see the Son of Man seated at the right side of the Almighty and coming with the clouds of heaven!"

10. **The religious leaders voted to put Jesus to death.**

    Mark 14:63-64 (page _____ in the New Testament): The High Priest tore his robes and said, "We don't need any more witnesses! You heard His blasphemy. What is your decision?" They all voted against Him: He was guilty and should be put to death.

11. **The religious leaders took Jesus to Pilate, the Roman Governor.**

    John 18:28-31 (page _____ in the New Testament): Early in the morning, Jesus was taken from Caiaphas' house to the governor's palace. The Jewish authorities did not go inside the palace, for they wanted to keep themselves ritually clean, in order to be able to eat the Passover meal. So Pilate went outside to them and asked, "What do you accuse this man of?" Their answer was, "We would not have brought Him to you if He had not committed a crime." Pilate said to them, "Then you yourselves take Him and try Him according to your own law." They replied, "We are not allowed to put anyone to death."

Part IV: Easter Celebration—God's Plan Fulfilled

12. Pilate asked Jesus, "Are You the King of the Jews?"

John 18:33-35 (page _____ in the New Testament): Pilate went back into the palace and called Jesus, "Are You the King of the Jews?" he asked Him. Jesus answered, "Does this question come from you or have others told you about Me?" Pilate replied, "Do You think I am a Jew? It was Your own people and the chief priests who handed You over to me. What have You done?"

13. Jesus told Pilate that His kingdom was not an earthly kingdom.

John 18:36-37(page _____ in the New Testament): Jesus said, "My kingdom does not belong to this world; if My kingdom belonged to this world, My followers would fight to keep Me from being handed over to the Jewish authorities. No, My kingdom does not belong here!" So Pilate asked Him, "Are You a King, then?" Jesus answered, "You say that I am a king. I was born and came into the world for this one purpose, to speak about the truth. Whoever belongs to the truth listens to Me."

14. Pilate had Jesus whipped to please the Jewish people.

John 19:1-5 (page _____ in the New Testament): Then Pilate took Jesus and had Him whipped. The soldiers made a crown out of thorny branches and put it on His head; then they put a purple robe on Him and came to Him and said, "Long live the King of the Jews!" And they went up and slapped Him. Pilate went back out once more and said to the crowd, "Look, I will bring Him out here to you to let you see that I cannot find any reason to condemn Him." So Jesus came out, wearing the crown of thorns and the purple robe. Pilate said to them, "Look! Here is the Man!"

15. The people wanted Jesus to be killed.

John 19:6-7 (page _____ in the New Testament): When the chief priests and the Temple guards saw Him, they shouted, "Crucify Him! Crucify Him!" Pilate said to them, "You take Him, then, and crucify Him. I find no reason to condemn Him." The crowd answered back, "We have a law that says He ought to die because He claimed to be the Son of God."

16. Pilate said that he had the power to kill Jesus or to set Him free.

John 19:8-10 (page _____ in the New Testament): When Pilate heard this, he was even more afraid. He went back into the palace and asked Jesus, "Where do You come from?" But Jesus did not answer. Pilate said to Him, "You will not speak to me? Remember, I have the authority to set You free and also to have You crucified."

17. Jesus responded.

John 19:11a (page _____ in the New Testament): Jesus answered, "You have authority over Me only because it was given to you by God."

18. Pilate wanted to set Jesus free.

John 19:12-14 (page _____ in the New Testament): When Pilate heard this, he tried to find a way to set Jesus free. But the crowd shouted back, "If you set Him free, that

God's Plan for Christian Living

means that you are not the Emperor's friend! Anyone who claims to be a king is a rebel against the Emperor!" When Pilate heard these words, he took Jesus outside and sat down on the judge's seat in the place called "The Stone Pavement." (In Hebrew the name is "Gabbatha.") It was then almost noon of the day before the Passover. Pilate said to the people, "Here is your King!"

19. The people shouted back to Pilate, "Kill Him!"

John 19:15 (page _____ in the New Testament): They shouted back, "Kill Him! Kill Him! Crucify Him!" Pilate asked them, "Do you want me to crucify your King?" The chief priests answered, "The only king we have is the Emperor!"

20. Pilate handed Jesus over.

John 19:16 (page _____ in the New Testament): Then Pilate handed Jesus to them to be crucified. So they took charge of Jesus.

Answer the following questions:

---

1. What did the High Priest ask Jesus?

   _____

2. What did Jesus answer?

   _____

Read #17 in the lesson. Jesus told Pilate that God gave Pilate authority over Him. This means that Jesus GAVE His life: No one could take it.

Do you believe Jesus gave His life for you? _____

DAILY BIBLE READINGS—Read from the Bible in your language and from the Good News Bible/Sunday School Bible:

Sunday	John 18:28-31
Monday	John 18:33-35
Tuesday	John 18:36-37
Wednesday	John 19:1-5
Thursday	John 19:6-7
Friday	John 19:8-11
Saturday	John 19:12-15

Part IV: Easter Celebration—God's Plan Fulfilled

Lesson 29

Jesus' Death on the Cross

Memory Verse: John 3:16 (page _____ in the New Testament): For God loved the world so much that He gave His only Son, so that everyone who believes in Him may not die but have eternal life.

1. **Jesus carried His own cross to a place called Golgotha, where the soldiers crucified Him.**

   John 19:17-18 (page _____ in the New Testament): He went out, carrying his cross to "The Place of the Skull," as it is called. (In Hebrew it is called "Golgotha.") There they crucified Him, and they also crucified two other men, one on each side, with Jesus between them.

2. **Pilate placed a sign on the cross of Jesus.**

   John 19:19-22 (page _____ in the New Testament): Pilate wrote a notice and had it put on the cross. "Jesus of Nazareth, the King of the Jews," is what he wrote. Many people read it, because the place where Jesus was crucified was not far from the city. The notice was written in Hebrew, Latin, and Greek. The chief priests said to Pilate, "Do not write 'The King of the Jews,' but rather, 'This Man said, I am the King of the Jews.'" Pilate answered, "What I have written stays written."

3. **The soldiers gambled for His robe.**

   John 19:23-24 (page _____ in the New Testament): After the soldiers had crucified Jesus, they took His clothes and divided them into four parts—one part for each soldier. They also took the robe, which was made of one piece of woven cloth without any seams in it. The soldiers said to one another, "Let's not tear it; let's throw dice to see who will get it." This happened in order to make the Scripture come true: "They divided My clothes among themselves and gambled for My robe." And this is what the soldiers did.

God's Plan for Christian Living

4. Jesus made seven statements while He was on the cross.

  i. Jesus prayed for the people who killed Him.

  Luke 23:34 (page _____ in the New Testament): Jesus said, "Forgive them, Father! They don't know what they are doing."

  ii. Jesus told John to care for His mother.

  John 19:25-27 (page _____ in the New Testament): Standing close to Jesus' cross were His mother, His mother's sister, Mary the wife of Clopas, and Mary Magdalene. Jesus saw His mother and the disciple He loved standing there; so He said to His mother, "He is your son." Then He said to the disciple, "She is your mother." From that time the disciple took her to live in his home.

  iii. Jesus forgave the robber who repented.

  Luke 23:39-43 (page _____ in the New Testament): One of the criminals hanging there hurled insults at Him: "Aren't You the Messiah? Save Yourself and us!" The other one, however, rebuked him, saying, "Don't you fear God? You received the same sentence He did. Ours, however, is only right, because we are getting what we deserve for what we did; but He has done no wrong." And he said to Jesus, "Remember me, Jesus, when You come as King!" Jesus said to him, "I promise you that today you will be in Paradise with Me."

  iv. Jesus was forsaken by God.

  Mark 15:33-34 (page _____ in the New Testament): At noon the whole country was covered with darkness, which lasted for three hours. At three o'clock Jesus cried out with a loud shout, "ELOI, ELOI, LEMA SABACHTHANI?" which means, "My God, My God, why did You abandon Me?"

  v. Jesus was thirsty.

  John 19:28-29 (page _____ in the New Testament): Jesus knew that by now everything had been completed; and in order to make the Scripture come true, He said, "I am thirsty." A bowl was there, full of cheap wine; so a sponge was soaked in the wine, put on a stalk of hyssop, and lifted up to His lips.

  vi. Jesus knew that His earthly ministry was finished.

  John 19:30 (page _____ in the New Testament): Jesus drank the wine and said, "It is finished!" Then He bowed His head and gave up His spirit.

  vii. Jesus GAVE His life.

  Luke 23:46 (page _____ in the New Testament): Jesus cried out in a loud voice, "Father! In Your hands I place My spirit!" He said this and died.

Part IV: Easter Celebration—God's Plan Fulfilled

5. **When Jesus died, many wonderful and strange things happened.**

   Matthew 27:45, 51-53 (page _____ in the New Testament): At noon the whole country was covered with darkness, which lasted for three hours. . . . Then the curtain hanging in the Temple was torn in two from top to bottom. The earth shook, the rocks split apart, the graves broke open, and many of God's people who had died were raised to life. They left the graves, and after Jesus rose from death, they went into the Holy City, where many people saw them.

6. **Some of the soldiers who crucified Jesus believed in Him.**

   Matthew 27:54 (page _____ in the New Testament): When the army officer and the soldiers with him who were watching Jesus saw the earthquake and everything else that happened, they were terrified and said, "He really was the Son of God!"

7. **Jesus was buried.**

   i. Joseph of Arimathea asked Pilate for the body of Jesus.

   Matthew 27:57-58 (page _____ in the New Testament): When it was evening, a rich man from Arimathea arrived; his name was Joseph, and he also was a disciple of Jesus. He went into the presence of Pilate and asked for the body of Jesus. Pilate gave orders for the body to be given to Joseph.

   ii. Joseph and Nicodemus buried Jesus.

   John 19:39-42 (page _____ in the New Testament): Nicodemus, who at first had gone to see Jesus at night, went with Joseph, taking with him about one hundred pounds of spices, a mixture of myrrh and aloes. The two men took Jesus' body and wrapped it in linen cloths with the spices according to the Jewish custom of preparing a body for burial. There was a garden in the place where Jesus had been put to death, and in it there was a new tomb where no one had ever been buried. Since it was the day before the Sabbath and because the tomb was close by, they placed Jesus' body there.

   iii. Mary Magdalene and the other Mary were watching.

   Mark 15:47 (page _____ in the New Testament): Mary Magdalene and Mary the mother of Jesus were watching and saw where the body of Jesus was placed.

   iv. The Pharisees asked Pilate to seal the tomb.

   Matthew 27:62-64 (page _____ in the New Testament): The next day, which was a Sabbath, the chief priests and the Pharisees met with Pilate and said, "Sir, we remember that while that liar was still alive He said, 'I will be raised to life three days later.' Give orders, then, for His tomb to be carefully guarded until the third day, so that His disciples will not be able to go and steal the body, and then tell the people that He was raised from death. This last lie would be even worse that the first one."

God's Plan for Christian Living

> v. Pilate ordered a seal and a guard for the tomb.
>
> *Matthew 27:65-66 (page _____ in the New Testament): "Take a guard," Pilate told them; "go and make the tomb as secure as you can." So they left and made the tomb secure by putting a seal on the stone and leaving the guard on watch.*

> *Romans 5:8 (page _____ in the New Testament): But God has shown us how much He loves us—it was while we were still sinners that Christ died for us!*

- What part did you have in Jesus' death? Does Jesus' death have any importance to you? If so, write what Jesus' death means to you:

  _____
  _____
  _____

If Jesus' death has no importance to you, carefully read this lesson again, then ask God to teach you the importance of Jesus' death.

> *The Crucifixion Story as told in the Gospels:*
>
> Matthew 27:32-56
>
> Mark 15:21-41
>
> Luke 23:26-49
>
> John 19:16-37

DAILY BIBLE READINGS—Read from the Bible in your language and from the Good News Bible/Sunday School Bible:

Sunday	Luke 23:32-38
Monday	John 19:25-27
Tuesday	Luke 23:39-43
Wednesday	Mark 15:33-34
Thursday	John 19:28-29
Friday	John 19:30
Saturday	Luke 23:44-49

Part IV: Easter Celebration—God's Plan Fulfilled

Lesson 30

The Lord Is Risen!

> *The LORD is risen!*
>
> *The LORD is risen indeed!*
>
> *HE is NOT here!*
>
> *The LORD is risen from the dead!*
>
> *Hallelujah! Hallelujah!*

1. **Early Sunday morning, two women went to the tomb of Jesus. They were special friends of Jesus.**

    Matthew 28:1 (page _____ in the New Testament): After the Sabbath, as Sunday morning was dawning, Mary Magdalene and the other Mary went to look at the tomb.

2. **An angel of the Lord came from heaven and rolled the stone away from the tomb.**

    Matthew 28:2-3 (page _____ in the New Testament): Suddenly there was a violent earthquake; an angel of the Lord came down from heaven, rolled the stone away, and sat on it. His appearance was like lightning, and his clothes were white as snow.

3. **The Roman guards were very frightened.**

    Matthew 28:4 (page _____ in the New Testament): The guards were so afraid that they trembled and became like dead men.

4. **The angel said to the women . . .**

    i. "You must not be afraid."

    ii. Jesus is NOT HERE—HE IS RISEN!

iii. You go tell His disciples that HE IS RISEN FROM THE DEAD!

Matthew 28:5-7 (page _____ in the New Testament): The angel spoke to the women. "You must not be afraid," he said. "I know you are looking for Jesus, who was crucified. He is not here; He has been raised, just as He said. Come here and see the place where He was lying. Go quickly now, and tell His disciples, 'He has been raised from death, and now He is going to Galilee ahead of you; there you will see Him!' Remember what I have told you."

5. The women were very excited! They ran to tell the disciples.

Matthew 28:8 (page _____ in the New Testament): So they left the tomb in a hurry, afraid and yet filled with joy, and ran to tell His disciples.

6. Jesus met with them.

Matthew 28:9-10 (page _____ in the New Testament): Suddenly, Jesus met them and said, "Peace be with you." They came up to Him, took hold of His feet, and worshiped Him. "Do not be afraid," Jesus said to them. "Go and tell My brothers to go to Galilee, and there they will see Me."

> *John 14:27 (page _____ in the New Testament): "Peace is what I leave with you;*
> *it is My own peace that I give you.*
> *I do not give it as the world does.*
> *Do not be worried and upset;*
> *do not be afraid."*

DAILY BIBLE READINGS—Read from the Bible in your language and from the Good News Bible/Sunday School Bible:

Sunday	Matthew 28:1-4
Monday	Matthew 28:5-8
Tuesday	Matthew 28:9-10
Wednesday	John 14:27
Thursday	John 11:25-26
Friday	2 Timothy 1:10
Saturday	John 6:40

Lesson 31

Jesus' Last Days on Earth

> *Memory Verse: Acts 1:8 (page _____ in the New Testament): "But when the Holy Spirit comes upon you, you will be filled with power, and you will be witnesses for Me in Jerusalem, in all of Judea and Samaria, and to the ends of the earth."*

Many people saw Jesus after His resurrection.

Jesus gave His friends important instructions.

Jesus went back to heaven.

1. **Thomas saw Jesus. He believed that Jesus was the Lord.**

    i. Thomas had not seen Jesus since His resurrection.

    John 20:24-25 (page _____ in the New Testament): One of the twelve disciples, Thomas (called the Twin), was not with them when Jesus came. So the other disciples told him, "We have seen the Lord!" Thomas said to them, "Unless I see the scars of the nails in His hands and put my finger on those scars and my hand in His side, I will not believe."

    ii. Thomas was with the other disciples when Jesus came and stood among them.

    John 20:26-27 (page _____ in the New Testament): A week later the disciples were together again indoors, and Thomas was with them. The doors were locked, but Jesus came and stood among them and said, "Peace be with you." Then He said to Thomas, "Put your finger here, and look at My hands, then reach out your hand and put it in My side. Stop your doubting, and believe!"

    iii. Thomas responded.

    John 20:28 (page _____ in the New Testament): Thomas answered Him, "My Lord and my God!"

    iv. Jesus spoke to Thomas.

    John 20:29 (page _____ in the New Testament): Jesus said to him, "Do you believe because you see Me? How happy are those who believe without seeing Me!"

God's Plan for Christian Living

2. **Jesus cooked breakfast for seven of His disciples.**

   John 21:9-13 (page _____ in the New Testament): When they stepped ashore, they saw a charcoal fire there with fish on it and some bread. Then Jesus said to them, "Bring some of the fish you have just caught." Simon Peter went aboard and dragged the net ashore full of big fish, a hundred and fifty-three in all; even though there were so many, still the net did not tear. Jesus said to them, "Come and eat." None of the disciples dared ask Him, "Who are You?" because they knew it was the Lord. So Jesus went over, took the bread, and gave it to them; He did the same with the fish.

3. **Jesus and Peter had a special talk.**

   John 21:15-17 (page _____ in the New Testament): After they had eaten, Jesus said to Simon Peter, "Simon, son of John, do you love Me more than these others do?" "Yes, Lord," he answered, "You know that I love You." Jesus said to him, "Take care of My lambs." A second time Jesus said to him, "Simon, son of John, do you love Me?" "Yes, Lord," he answered, "You know that I love You." Jesus said to him, "Take care of My sheep." A third time Jesus said, "Simon, son of John, do you love Me?" Peter became sad because Jesus asked him the third time, "Do you love Me?" and so he said to Him, "Lord, You know everything; You know that I love you!" Jesus said to him, "Take care of My sheep."

   i. Peter had denied Jesus three times.

   ii. Jesus asked Peter three times, "Do you love Me?"

   iii. Peter answered Jesus three times, "Yes, Lord!"

   iv. Jesus wanted Peter to know that he was forgiven.

4. **All the promises about Jesus came true in His life, in His death, and in His resurrection.**

   Luke 24:44-46 (page _____ in the New Testament): Then He said to them, "These are the very things I told you about while I was still with you: everything written about Me in the Law of Moses, the writings of the prophets, and the Psalms had to come true." Then He opened their minds to understand the Scriptures, and said to them, "This is what is written: the Messiah must suffer and must rise from death three days later."

5. **Jesus gave His disciples a special command.**

   Luke 24:47-49 (page _____ in the New Testament): "And in His (Jesus')name the message about repentance and the forgiveness of sins must be preached to all nations, beginning in Jerusalem. You are witnesses of these things. And I Myself will send upon you what My Father has promised. But you must wait in the city until the power from above comes down upon you."

   Matthew 28:18-20 (page _____ in the New Testament): Jesus drew near and said to them, "I have been given all authority in heaven and on earth. Go, then, to all peoples everywhere and make them My disciples: baptize them in the name of the Father, the

Son, and the Holy Spirit, and teach them to obey everything I have commanded you. And I will be with you always, to the end of the age."

Acts 1:8 (page _____ in the New Testament): "But when the Holy Spirit comes upon you, you will be filled with power, and you will be witnesses for Me in Jerusalem, in all of Judea and Samaria, and to the ends of the earth."

6. Jesus went back to heaven.

Luke 24:50-53 (page _____ in the New Testament): Then He led them out of the city as far as Bethany, where He raised His hands and blessed them. As He was blessing them, He departed from them and was taken up into heaven. They worshiped Him and went back into Jerusalem, filled with great joy, and spent all their time in the Temple giving thanks to God.

Answer the following questions:

1. Thomas had to see the scars of Jesus to believe Jesus was alive. What has helped you to believe that Jesus is alive?

   _____
   _____
   _____

2. Did Peter know that Jesus had forgiven Him? _____

3. Do you know that Jesus has forgiven you? _____

DAILY BIBLE READINGS—Read from the Bible in your language and from the Good News Bible/Sunday School Bible:

Sunday	John 20:24-25
Monday	John 20:26-29
Tuesday	John 21:1-6
Wednesday	John 21:7-10
Thursday	John 21:11-14
Friday	John 21:15-16
Saturday	John 21:17-19

Part V:

The Christian Life—Growing through Obedience

Lesson 32

Abraham Obeyed God

Memory verse: Proverbs 3:5-7 (page _____ in the Old Testament): Trust in the LORD with all your heart. Never rely on what you think you know. Remember the LORD in everything you do, and He will show you the right way. Never let yourself think that you are wiser than you are; simply obey the LORD and refuse to do wrong.

God told Abraham to go to another country. Abraham trusted God. He obeyed God.

Hebrews 11:8-10 (page _____ in the New Testament): It was faith that made Abraham obey when God called him to go out to a country which God had promised to give him. He left his own country without knowing where he was going. By faith he lived as a foreigner in the country that God had promised him. He lived in tents, as did Isaac and Jacob, who received the same promise from God. For Abraham was waiting for the city which God has designed and built, the city with permanent foundations.

Abraham could not understand God's promise to him. Abraham trusted God and obeyed God.

God made man free to choose. Man can choose to trust in God or he can choose not to trust in God. Man can choose to obey God or not to obey God.

Trusting in God is choosing God's way for your life. People cannot understand how the death and resurrection of Jesus can give them eternal life. People must trust God for eternal life. Christians choose God's way for their lives. Christians trust God for eternal life. Christians obey God.

God's Plan for Christian Living

Answer the following questions in your own words:

1. Write the meaning of *faith:*

   _____

   _____

2. Write the meaning of *believe:*

   _____

   _____

3. Why did Abraham obey God?

   _____

   _____

4. Why do Christians obey God?

   _____

   _____

DAILY BIBLE READINGS—Read from the Bible in your language and from the Good News Bible/Sunday School Bible:

Sunday	Acts 7:2-3
Monday	Galatians 3:6-7
Tuesday	Galatians 3:8-9
Wednesday	Romans 4:1-3
Thursday	Genesis 15:6
Friday	James 2:23
Saturday	Genesis 21:1-3

Part V: The Christian Life—Growing through Obedience

Lesson 33

Abraham Trusted God When It Seemed Impossible

Memory Verse: Genesis 18:14a (page ____ in the Old Testament): "Is anything too hard for the LORD?"

God promised Abraham and Sarah a son. Many, many years passed, and the son had not been born. Abraham and Sarah thought it was impossible for them to have a son. They were too old.

God repeated His promise to Abraham and Sarah. They continued to trust God. When Abraham was one hundred years old and Sarah was ninety, the promised son was born. They named him Isaac.

Hebrews 11:11 (page ____ in the New Testament): It was faith that made Abraham able to become a father, even though he was too old and Sarah herself could not have children. He trusted God to keep His promise.

God gives us many promises in His Word/Bible:

i. God promises ETERNAL LIFE to those who trust in Him.

   John 3:16 (page ____ in the New Testament): For God loved the world so much that He gave His only Son, so that everyone who believes in Him may not die but have eternal life.

ii. God promises PEACE to those who trust in Him.

   Isaiah 26:3 (page ____ in the Old Testament): You, LORD, give perfect peace to those who keep their purpose firm and put their trust in you.

iii. God promises STRENGTH to those who trust in Him.

   Psalm 73:26 (page ____ in the Old Testament): My mind and my body may grow weak, but God is my strength; He is all I ever need.

115

God's Plan for Christian Living

iv. God promises WISDOM to those who trust in Him.

James 1:5-6 (page _____ in the New Testament): But if any of you lack wisdom, he should pray to God, who will give it to him; because God gives generously and graciously to all. But when you pray, you must believe and not doubt at all. Whoever doubts is like a wave in the sea that is driven and blown about by the wind.

Sometimes people think it is impossible for God to keep His promises.

Sometimes people think it is impossible for God to keep His promises to me.

Sometimes people think it is impossible for God to keep His promises to me because my situation is so difficult.

BUT GOD IS FAITHFUL!

- GOD does HIS part: He makes promises to me. He keeps His promises.
- I MUST DO MY PART: I must believe God. I must know His promises. I must believe His promises. I must obey God.

> Answer the following questions:

1. Abraham believed God. Do you believe God? _____

2. Abraham knew God's promises. Do you know God's promises? _____

3. Abraham believed God's promises. Do you believe God's promises? _____

4. Abraham obeyed God. Will you obey God? _____

DAILY BIBLE READINGS—Read from the Bible in your language and from the Good News Bible/Sunday School Bible:

Sunday	Hebrews 11:11
Monday	John 3:16
Tuesday	Isaiah 26:3
Wednesday	Psalm 73:26
Thursday	James 1:5-6
Friday	2 Peter 1:3-4
Saturday	Luke 1:37

Lesson 34

Abraham Obeyed God When It Seemed Impossible

Memory Verse: Genesis 22:12b (page _____ in the Old Testament): "Now I know that you honor and obey God, because you have not kept back your only son from Him."

God told Abraham to go to another country. Abraham obeyed God. God promised Abraham and Sarah a son. Abraham and Sarah trusted God to keep His promise. God gave Abraham and Sarah a son. They named him Isaac.

Genesis 22:1-14 (page _____ in the Old Testament): Some time later, God tested Abraham; He called to him, "Abraham!" and Abraham answered, "Yes, here I am!" "Take your son," God said, "your only son, Isaac, whom you love so much, and go to the land of Moriah. There on a mountain that I will show you, offer him as a sacrifice to Me." Early the next morning Abraham cut some wood for the sacrifice, loaded his donkey, and took Isaac and two servants with him. They started out for the place that God had told him about. On the third day Abraham saw the place in the distance. Then he said to the servants, "Stay here with the donkey. The boy and I will go over there and worship, and then we will come back to you." Abraham made Isaac carry the wood for the sacrifice, and he himself carried a knife and live coals for starting the fire. As they walked along together, Isaac spoke up, "Father!" He answered, "Yes, my son?" Isaac asked, "I see that you have the coals and the wood, but where is the lamb for the sacrifice?" Abraham answered, "God Himself will provide one."

And the two of them walked on together. When they came to the place which God had told him about, Abraham built an altar and arranged the wood on it. He tied up his son and placed him on the altar, on top of the wood. Then he picked up the knife to kill him. But the angel of the LORD called to him from heaven, "Abraham, Abraham!" He answered, "Yes, here I am." "Don't hurt the boy or do anything to him," He said. "Now I know that you honor and obey God because you have not kept back your only son from Him." Abraham looked around and saw a ram caught in a bush by its horns. He went and got it and offered it as a burnt offering instead of his son. Abraham named that place "The LORD Provides." And even today people say, "On the LORD's mountain He provides."

God's Plan for Christian Living

Abraham lived close to God. Abraham listened to God.

Abraham loved his son, Isaac, very much, but he loved God more than he loved Isaac. Abraham had to choose to obey God or to disobey God. Abraham chose to obey God.

God provided Abraham's needs when Abraham obeyed God. Abraham trusted God and God provided (a lamb) for the sacrifice. God made a great nation from Abraham and his descendants.

Genesis 22:18 (page _____ in the Old Testament): "All the nations will ask Me to bless them as I have blessed your descendants—all because you obeyed My command."

Answer the following questions:

1. Do you love God enough to trust Him? _____

2. Do you love God more than you love your family? _____

3. Do you love God more than you love your work? _____

4. Do you love God enough to obey Him in every situation? _____

5. Do you trust Him to provide for your needs in every situation? _____

DAILY BIBLE READINGS—Read from the Bible in your language and from the Good News Bible/Sunday School Bible:

Sunday	Hebrews 11:17-19
Monday	Genesis 22:15-19
Tuesday	Hebrews 6:13-15
Wednesday	Psalm 37:3-6
Thursday	Psalm 40:1-3
Friday	Psalm 40:4-5
Saturday	Psalm 40:6-8

Part V: The Christian Life—Growing through Obedience

Lesson 35

Moses Obeyed God after Moses Made Excuses

Memory Verse: Exodus 3:11 (page ____ in the Old Testament): But Moses said to God, "I am nobody. How can I go to the king and bring the Israelites out of Egypt?"

Moses was Hebrew. The Hebrews had become slaves of the Egyptians. Moses saw an Egyptian kill a Hebrew. When no one was looking, Moses killed the Egyptian. Moses lived in another country (Midian) forty years to save his own life. (Read Exodus 2:11-15, page ____ in the Old Testament.)

God had a plan for Moses to help the Hebrew people. God called to Moses from a burning bush.

Exodus 3:10 (page ____ in the Old Testament): "Now I am sending you to the king of Egypt so that you can lead My people out of his country."

Moses made excuses for not obeying God. God answered Moses.

Moses' Excuses	God's Answers
1. "I am nobody."	1. "I will be with you."
Exodus 3:11 (page ____ in the Old Testament): But Moses said to God, "I am nobody. How can I go to the king and bring the Israelites out of Egypt?"	*Exodus 3:12 (page ____ in the Old Testament): God answered, "I will be with you, and when you bring the people out of Egypt, you will worship Me on this mountain. That will be the proof that I have sent you."*

2. "I don't know Your name." *Exodus 3:13 (page ____ in the Old Testament): But Moses replied, "When I go to the Israelites and say to them, 'The God of your ancestors sent me to you,' they will ask me, 'What is His name?' So what can I tell them?"*	2. "My name is I AM." *Exodus 3:14-15 (page ____ in the Old Testament): God said, "I am who I am. You must tell them: 'The One who is called I AM has sent me to you.' Tell the Israelites that I, the LORD, the God of their ancestors, the God of Abraham, Isaac, and Jacob, have sent you to them. This is My name forever; this is what all future generations are to call Me."*
3. "The Israelites may not believe me." *Exodus 4:1 (page ____ in the Old Testament): Then Moses answered the LORD, "But suppose the Israelites do not believe me and will not listen to what I say. What shall I do if they say that You did not appear to me?"*	3. "You will show My miracles." *Exodus 4:5 (page ____ in the Old Testament): The LORD said, "Do this to prove to the Israelites that the LORD, the God of their ancestors, the God of Abraham, Isaac, and Jacob, has appeared to you."*
4. "I am not a good speaker." *Exodus 4:10 (page ____ in the Old Testament): But Moses said, "No, LORD, don't send me. I have never been a good speaker, and I haven't become one since You began to speak to me. I am a poor speaker, slow and hesitant."*	4. "I will tell you what to say." *Exodus 4:12 (page ____ in the Old Testament): "Now, go! I will help you speak, and I will tell you what to say."*
5. "Let somebody else go." *Exodus 4:13 (page ____ in the Old Testament): But Moses answered, "No LORD, please send someone else."*	5. "I will help you." *Exodus 4:15b-17 (page ____ in the Old Testament): "I will help both of you to speak, and I will tell you both what to do . . . . Take this walking stick with you; for with it you will perform miracles."*

Moses obeyed God. He went back to Egypt. He led his people to the land God had promised them. God helped Moses. God did everything He had promised.

God chooses us to show His love to people. Sometimes we make excuses. We do not understand God. We ask Him questions. We think we cannot do what He wants us to do.

God answers our excuses. He helps us when we do not understand. He gives us what we need to obey Him. God uses us when we choose to obey Him.

Answer the following questions:

1. Do you ever think that you are a "nobody"? _____

2. Do you ever think that you do not know God? _____

3. Do you ever think that people will not believe you? _____

4. Do you think that God will help you? _____

> *Philippians 4:19-20 (page ____ in the New Testament): And with all His abundant wealth through Christ Jesus, my God will supply all your needs. To our God and Father be the glory forever and ever! Amen.*

DAILY BIBLE READINGS—Read from the Bible in your language and from the Good News Bible/Sunday School Bible:

Sunday	Exodus 3:7-12
Monday	Exodus 3:13-17
Tuesday	Exodus 3:18-20
Wednesday	Exodus 4:1-5
Thursday	Exodus 4:6-9
Friday	Exodus 4:10-11, 15-17
Saturday	Exodus 3:1-6

Lesson 36

Joshua Led the People to Obey God

Memory Verse: Joshua 1:16 (page ____ in the Old Testament): They answered Joshua, "We will do everything you have told us and will go anywhere you send us."

God chose Joshua to lead His people into the land He had promised them. The people had to cross a river to enter the Promised Land. The river was in flood.

1. **Joshua told the people what God had said.**

   Joshua 3:13 (page ____ in the Old Testament): "When the priests who carry the Covenant Box of the LORD of all the earth put their feet in the water, the Jordan will stop flowing, and the water coming downstream will pile up in one place."

2. **The people obeyed God. God did everything He had promised the people.**

   Joshua 3:14-17 (page ____ in the Old Testament): It was harvest time, and the river was in flood. When the people left the camp to cross the Jordan, the priests were ahead of them, carrying the Covenant Box. As soon as the priests stepped into the river, the water stopped flowing and piled up, far upstream at Adam, the city beside Zarethan. The flow downstream to the Dead Sea was completely cut off, and the people were able to cross over near Jericho. While the people walked across on dry ground, the priests carrying the LORD's Covenant Box stood on dry ground in the middle of the Jordan until all the people had crossed over.

Joshua obeyed God. He led the people to obey God. The people had to obey God before they saw God's promise fulfilled. When they obeyed God, God did everything He had promised.

God's promises are for us today. Sometimes what God tells us to do seems impossible. But as we obey God, He keeps His promises.

Part V: The Christian Life—Growing through Obedience

God's Instructions to Moses	God's Promises
1. Do not be afraid or discouraged.	1. God is with you. *Joshua 1:9b (page ____ in the Old Testament): "Do not be afraid or discouraged, for I, the LORD your God, am with you wherever you go."*
2. Put your trust in God.	2. God gives perfect peace. *Isaiah 26:3 (page ____ in the Old Testament): "You, LORD, give perfect peace to those who keep their purpose firm and put their trust in You."*
3. Tell people about God's love.	3. God will be with you. *Matthew 28:19-20 (page ____ in the New Testament): "Go, then, to all peoples everywhere and make them My disciples: baptize them in the name of the Father, the Son, and the Holy Spirit, and teach them to obey everything I have commanded you. And I will be with you always, to the end of the age."*

> *Joshua 23:14b (page ____ in the Old Testament): "Every one of you knows in his heart and soul that the LORD your God has given you all the good things that He promised. Every promise He made has been kept; not one has failed."*

1. When has God kept His promise to you? _____

2. How did God keep His promise to you? _____

DAILY BIBLE READINGS—Read from the Bible in your language and from the Good News Bible/Sunday School Bible:

Sunday	Joshua 1:1-3
Monday	Joshua 1:7-9
Tuesday	Joshua 1:16-17
Wednesday	Joshua 3:1-4a
Thursday	Joshua 3:7-8
Friday	Joshua 3:13-17
Saturday	Joshua 23:14b

Lesson 37

Gideon Obeyed God When He Was Afraid

Memory Verse: Judges 6:16a (page ____ in the Old Testament): The LORD answered, "You can do it because I will help you."

Joshua led God's people into the Promised Land. Soon the Israelites turned away from God. They did not worship God. They worshiped other gods.

The Lord let the people of Midian rule over the Israelites. The Israelites asked God for help.

1. **God answered the people.**

    Judges 6:8b-10 (page ____ in the Old Testament): "I brought you out of slavery in Egypt. I rescued you from the Egyptians and from the people who fought you here in this land. I drove them out as you advanced, and I gave you their land. I told you that I am the LORD your God and that you should not worship the gods of the Amorites, whose land you are now living in. But you have not listened to Me."

2. **God chose Gideon to rescue His people. God gave Gideon orders.**

    Judges 6:14 (page ____ in the Old Testament): Then the LORD ordered him, "Go with all your great strength and rescue Israel from the Midianites. I Myself am sending you."

3. **Gideon replied.**

    Judges 6:15 (page ____ in the Old Testament): Gideon replied, "But LORD, how can I rescue Israel? My clan is the weakest in the tribe of Manasseh, and I am the least important member of my family."

4. **The Lord answered.**

    Judges 6:16 (page ____ in the Old Testament): The Lord answered, "You can do it because I will help you. You will crush the Midianites as easily as if they were only one man."

Judges 6:25-26 (page _____ in the Old Testament): The LORD told Gideon, "Take your father's bull and another bull seven years old, tear down your father's altar to Baal, and cut down the symbol of the goddess Asherah, which is beside it. Build a well-constructed altar to the LORD your God on top of this mound. Then take the second bull and burn it whole as an offering, using for firewood the symbol of Asherah you have cut down."

5. Gideon obeyed God.

Judges 6:27 (page _____ in the Old Testament): So Gideon took ten of his servants and did what the LORD had told him. He was too afraid of his family and the people in the town to do it by day, so he did it at night.

God chose Gideon to rescue His people. God told Gideon to tear down the altars to other gods. Gideon was afraid of the people. He was afraid the people might kill him if he destroyed the altars. Gideon obeyed God.

You can read more about Gideon in Judges 6, 7, and 8 (pages _____ in the Old Testament).

Answer the following questions:

1. Have you ever been afraid to obey God? _____

2. Did you obey God? _____

DAILY BIBLE READINGS—Read from the Bible in your language and from the Good News Bible/Sunday School Bible:

Sunday	Judges 6:1-2
Monday	Judges 6:3-6
Tuesday	Judges 6:7-10
Wednesday	Judges 6:11-12
Thursday	Judges 6:14-16
Friday	Judges 6:25-27
Saturday	Judges 6:28-32

Lesson 38

Saul Chose Not to Obey God

> *Memory Verse: 1 Samuel 12:24 (page _____ in the Old Testament): "Obey the LORD and serve Him faithfully with all your heart. Remember the great things He has done for you."*

Samuel was judge over Israel. The leaders of Israel asked Samuel to appoint a king to rule over them so that they would have a king as other countries had. Samuel asked the Lord for guidance. The Lord told Samuel to give the people a king. (Read 1 Samuel 8, page _____ in the Old Testament.)

1. **The Lord chose a young man named Saul from the tribe of Benjamin.**

    1 Samuel 9:15-16a (page _____ in the Old Testament): Now on the previous day the LORD had told Samuel, "Tomorrow about this time I will send you a man from the tribe of Benjamin; anoint him as ruler of my people Israel."

2. **Samuel anointed Saul as the first king of Israel.**

    1 Samuel 10:1a (page _____ in the Old Testament): Then Samuel took a jar of olive oil and poured it on Saul's head, kissed him, and said, "The LORD anoints you as ruler of His people Israel. You will rule His people and protect them from all their enemies."

3. **Samuel gave Saul the Lord's instructions.**

    1 Samuel 10:8 (page _____ in the Old Testament): "You will go ahead of me to Gilgal, where I will meet you and offer burnt sacrifices and fellowship sacrifices. Wait there seven days until I come and tell you what to do."

4. **Saul disobeyed the Lord.**

    1 Samuel 13:8-12 (page _____ in the Old Testament): He waited seven days for Samuel, as Samuel had instructed him to do, but Samuel still had not come to Gilgal. The people began to desert Saul, so he said to them, "Bring me the burnt sacrifices and the fellowship sacrifices." He offered a burnt sacrifice, and just as he was finishing, Samuel arrived. Saul went out to meet him and welcome him, but Samuel said, "What have

Part V: The Christian Life—Growing through Obedience

you done?" Saul answered, "The people were deserting me, and you had not come when you said you would; besides that, the Philistines are gathering at Michmash. So I thought, the Philistines are going to attack me here in Gilgal, and I have not tried to win the LORD's favor. So I felt I had to offer a sacrifice."

5. Saul was rejected as king.

1 Samuel 13:13-14 (page ____ in the Old Testament): "That was a foolish thing to do," Samuel answered. "You have not obeyed the command the LORD your God gave you. If you had obeyed, He would have let you and your descendants rule over Israel forever. But now your rule will not continue. Because you have disobeyed Him, the LORD will find the kind of man He wants and make Him ruler of His people."

God wants His people to obey Him. God's people do not always obey Him. If we ask God, He will forgive us when we do not obey Him.

Answer the following questions:

1. Do you always obey God? _____

2. Do you ever disobey God? _____

3. Do you ask God to forgive you when you disobey Him? _____

> *1 Samuel 15:22-23a (page ____ in the Old Testament): Samuel said, "Which does the LORD prefer: obedience or offerings and sacrifices? It is better to obey Him than to sacrifice the best sheep to Him. Rebellion against Him is as bad as witchcraft, and arrogance is as sinful as idolatry."*

DAILY BIBLE READINGS—Read from the Bible in your language and from the Good News Bible/Sunday School Bible:

Sunday	1 Samuel 12:24
Monday	1 Samuel 15:22-23a
Tuesday	Joshua 24:22-24
Wednesday	Acts 5:27-29
Thursday	Deuteronomy 4:27-30
Friday	1 Peter 1:22-23
Saturday	Psalm 51:10-13

Lesson 39

Elijah Obeyed God

> *Memory Verse: 1 Kings 18:39b (page _____ in the Old Testament): "The LORD is God; the LORD alone is God!"*

Ahab was a corrupt king of Israel. He allowed the worship of the idol, Baal. The temples of Baal worship were centers of evil.

Elijah was a prophet of God. He was a courageous spokesman for God. He warned the people not to worship idols. He warned the people not to disobey God.

1. **Elijah addressed King Ahab.**

   1 Kings 18:18b (page _____ in the Old Testament): "You are disobeying the Lord's commands and worshiping the idols of Baal."

2. **King Ahab responded.**

   1 Kings 18:20 (page _____ in the Old Testament): Ahab summoned all the Israelites and the prophets of Baal to meet at Mount Carmel.

3. **Elijah asked the people, "How much longer will it take?"**

   1 Kings 18:21-24 (page _____ in the Old Testament): Elijah went up to the people and said, "How much longer will it take you to make up your minds? If the Lord is God, worship Him; but if Baal is God, worship him!" But the people didn't say a word. Then Elijah said, "I am the only prophet of the Lord still left, but there are 450 prophets of Baal. Bring two bulls; let the prophets of Baal take one, kill it, cut it in pieces and put it on the wood—but don't light the fire. I will do the same with the other bull. Then let the prophets of Baal pray to their god, and I will pray to the Lord, and the one who answers by sending fire—He is God."

4. **Elijah told the prophets of Baal to make their sacrifice first. They made their sacrifice. They prayed to Baal. Baal did not answer.**

5. **Elijah prepared for his sacrifice to the Lord.**

Part V: The Christian Life—Growing through Obedience

1 Kings 18:30, 36-37 (page ____ in the Old Testament): Then Elijah said to the people, "Come closer to me," and they all gathered around him. He set about repairing the altar of the Lord which had been torn down. . . . At the hour of the afternoon sacrifice the prophet Elijah approached the altar and prayed, "O Lord, the God of Abraham, Isaac, and Jacob, prove now that You are the God of Israel and that I am Your servant and have done all this at Your command. Answer me, Lord, answer me, so that this people will know that You, the Lord, are God and that You are bringing them back to Yourself."

6. **The Lord answered Elijah.**

    1 Kings 18:38 (page ____ in the Old Testament): The Lord sent fire down, and it burned up the sacrifice, the wood, and the stones, scorched the earth and dried up the water in the trench.

7. **The people responded.**

    1 Kings 18:39 (page ____ in the Old Testament): When the people saw this, they threw themselves on the ground and exclaimed, "The Lord is God; the Lord alone is God!"

Elijah obeyed God. He gave the people God's messages. The people learned that the Lord alone is God.

Answer the following questions:

1. What was God's message that Elijah gave to the people? _____
   _____

2. Did the people believe Elijah's message? _____

3. Do you believe the LORD is God? _____

DAILY BIBLE READINGS—Read from the Bible in your language and from the Good News Bible/Sunday School Bible:

Sunday	1 Kings 18:38-39
Monday	1 Kings 19:1-2
Tuesday	1 Kings 19:3-4
Wednesday	1 Kings 19:5-6
Thursday	1 Kings 19:7-9
Friday	1 Kings 19:10
Saturday	1 Kings 19:11-12

God's Plan for Christian Living

Lesson 40

Jonah Tried to Disobey God

> *Memory Verse: Jonah 2:2 (page _____ in the Old Testament): "In my distress, O LORD, I called to You and You answered me."*

Jonah was a statesman from Israel. He was a prophet of God. God told Jonah to take His message to the people of Nineveh. God told Jonah to tell the people that their city would be destroyed in forty days because the people were very wicked. Jonah did not want to obey God. He fled in the opposite direction. He did not want to share God's love with the enemies of his country, Israel. He wanted the people of Nineveh to be destroyed.

1. **God spoke to Jonah again.**

    Jonah 3:1-2 (page _____ in the Old Testament): Once again the Lord spoke to Jonah. He said, "Go to Nineveh, that great city, and proclaim to the people the message I have given you."

2. **Jonah obeyed God.**

    Jonah 3:3-4 (page _____ in the Old Testament): So Jonah obeyed the Lord and went to Nineveh, a city so large that it took three days to walk through it. Jonah started through the city, and after walking a whole day, he proclaimed, "In forty days Nineveh will be destroyed."

3. **The people of Nineveh believed God's message.**

    Jonah 3:5-9 (page _____ in the Old Testament): The people of Nineveh believed God's message. So they decided that everyone should fast, and all the people, from the greatest to the least, put on sackcloth to show that they had repented. When the king of Nineveh heard about it, he got up from his throne, took off his robe, put on sackcloth, and sat down in ashes. He sent out a proclamation to the people of Nineveh: "This is an order from the king and his officials: No one is to eat or drink anything; all persons, cattle, and sheep are forbidden to eat or drink. All persons and animals must wear sackcloth. Everyone must pray earnestly to God and must give up his wicked behavior and his evil actions. Perhaps God will change His mind; perhaps He will stop being angry, and we will not die."

4. God forgave the people. He did not punish them.

Jonah 3:10 (page ____ in the Old Testament): God saw what they did; He saw that they had given up their wicked behavior. So He changed His mind and did not punish them as He had said He would.

Our God is a God of love and forgiveness. He does not want to punish and destroy any people. God wants to forgive and save all people of the world.

Answer the following questions:

1. Do you want all people of the world to know God's love and forgiveness? _____

2. Do you want your enemies to know God's love and forgiveness? _____

3. Do you know God's love and forgiveness? _____

4. Have you, personally, experienced God's love and forgiveness? _____

DAILY BIBLE READINGS—Read from the Bible in your language and from the Good News Bible/Sunday School Bible:

Sunday	Daniel 9:9
Monday	Psalm 103:8-10
Tuesday	Psalm 103:11-12
Wednesday	1 John 1:8-10
Thursday	Psalm 133:1
Friday	Psalm 128:1
Saturday	Jonah 2:8-9

Lesson 41

Daniel Obeyed God

> *Memory Verse: Acts 5:29b (page _____ in the New Testament): "We must obey God, not men."*

The kingdom of Babylon conquered the kingdom of Judah. Some of the young men from the kingdom of Judah were taken to Babylon to serve in the royal court. The young men had to be handsome, intelligent, well-trained, quick to learn, and free from physical defects. Daniel was one of these young men. Daniel became one of the most important leaders in Babylon. God gave Daniel special knowledge and skills. Daniel did better work than the other leaders.

Daniel continued to worship the Lord God.

Read Daniel 1 (page _____ in the Old Testament). The other leaders were jealous of Daniel. They had a plan to hurt him. They asked King Darius to issue an order. The order was that no one pray except to the king.

1. **Daniel did not obey the king's order. Daniel continued to pray to the Lord God.**

   Daniel 6:10 (page _____ in the Old Testament): When Daniel learned that the order had been signed, he went home. In an upstairs room of his house there were windows that faced toward Jerusalem. There, just as he had always done, he knelt down at the open windows and prayed to God three times a day.

2. **Daniel's enemies saw him praying to God. They told the king.**

   Daniel 6:11-13 (page _____ in the Old Testament): When Daniel's enemies observed him praying to God, all of them went together to the king to accuse Daniel. They said, "Your Majesty, you signed an order that for the next thirty days anyone who requested anything from any god or from any man except you, would be thrown into a pit filled with lions." The king replied, "Yes, that is a strict order, a law of the Medes and Persians, which cannot be changed." Then they said to the king, "Daniel, one of the exiles from Judah, does not respect Your Majesty or obey the order you issued. He prays regularly three times a day."

3. **The king was upset, but he could not save Daniel.**

   Daniel 6:14-15 (page _____ in the Old Testament): When the king heard this, he was upset and did his best to find some way to rescue Daniel. He kept trying until sunset. Then the men came back to the king and said to him, "Your Majesty knows that according to the laws of the Medes and Persians no order which the king issues can be changed."

4. **The king ordered that Daniel be thrown into the pit filled with lions.**

   Daniel 6:16-17 (page _____ in the Old Testament): So the king gave orders for Daniel to be taken and thrown into the pit filled with lions. He said to Daniel, "May your God, whom you serve so loyally, rescue you." A stone was put over the mouth of the pit, and the king placed his own royal seal and the seal of his noblemen on the stone, so that no one could rescue Daniel.

5. **Daniel could have been killed by the lions, BUT he was not hurt!**

   Daniel 6:19-23 (page _____ in the Old Testament): At dawn the king got up and hurried to the pit. When he got there, he called out anxiously, "Daniel, servant of the living God! Was the God you serve so loyally able to save you from the lions?" Daniel answered, "May Your Majesty live forever! God sent His angel to shut the mouths of the lions so that they would not hurt me. He did this because He knew that I was innocent and because I have not wronged you, Your Majesty." The king was overjoyed and gave orders for Daniel to be pulled up out of the pit. So they pulled him up and saw that he had not been hurt at all, for he trusted God.

   > *Daniel 6:25-27 (page _____ in the Old Testament): Then King Darius wrote to the people of all nations, races, and languages on earth: "Greetings! I command that throughout my empire everyone should fear and respect Daniel's God. He is a living God, and He will rule forever. His kingdom will never be destroyed, and His power will never come to an end. He saves and rescues; He performs wonders and miracles in heaven and on earth. He saved Daniel from being killed by the lions."*

> Answer the following questions:

1. Was it dangerous for Daniel to pray to God? _____

2. Today, is it dangerous for the people of all nations, races, and languages on earth to pray to God? _____

3. Is it dangerous for you to pray to God? _____

DAILY BIBLE READINGS—Read from the Bible in your language and from the Good News Bible/Sunday School Bible:

Sunday	Galatians 5:16-18
Monday	Galatians 5:19-21
Tuesday	Galatians 5:22-26
Wednesday	Galatians 6:1-3
Thursday	Galatians 6:4-6
Friday	Galatians 6:7-8
Saturday	Galatians 6:9-10

Part V: The Christian Life—Growing through Obedience

Lesson 42

Esther Obeyed and God Saved Her People

Memory Verse: Esther 4:16b (page _____ in the Old Testament): "After that, I will go to the king, even though it is against the law. If I must die for doing it, I will die."

Esther was a Jewish orphan. She was adopted by her cousin, Mordecai. She was reared as his own daughter. Mordecai was a high official in the government. Esther became a Persian queen.

King Xerxes made Haman his prime minister. King Xerxes ordered all the officials to show their respect to Haman by kneeling and bowing to him. Mordecai worshiped God. He did not bow to Haman.

Haman was very angry. He learned that Mordecai was a Jew. He made plans to kill every Jew in the Persian Empire. King Xerxes did not know Queen Esther was a Jew. He allowed Haman to proceed with his plans.

1. **The Jews learned about Haman's plans.**

    Esther 4:1-3 (page _____ in the Old Testament): When Mordecai learned of all that had been done, he tore his clothes in anguish. Then he dressed in sackcloth, covered his head with ashes, and walked through the city, wailing loudly and bitterly, until he came to the entrance of the palace. He did not go in because no one wearing sackcloth was allowed inside. Throughout all the provinces wherever the king's proclamation was made known, there was loud mourning among the Jews. They fasted, wept, wailed, and most of them put on sackcloth and lay in ashes.

2. **God had a plan to save His people. He chose Mordecai and Queen Esther to accomplish His plan. Mordecai sent Queen Esther a message.**

    Esther 4:8 (page _____ in the Old Testament): He gave Hathach a copy of the proclamation that had been issued in Susa, ordering the destruction of the Jews. Mordecai asked him to take it to Esther, explain the situation to her, and have her go and plead with the king and beg him to have mercy on her people.

God's Plan for Christian Living

3. **Queen Esther sent Mordecai a reply.**

   Esther 4:11 (page ____ in the Old Testament): "If anyone, man or woman, goes to the inner courtyard and sees the king without being summoned, that person must die. That is the law; everyone, from the king's advisers to the people in the provinces, knows that. There is only one way to get around this law: if the king holds out his gold scepter to someone, then that person's life is spared. But it has been a month since the king sent for me."

4. **Mordecai warned Queen Esther.**

   Esther 4:12-14 (page ____ in the Old Testament): When Mordecai received Esther's message, he sent her this warning: "Don't imagine that you are safer than any other Jew just because you are in the royal palace. If you keep quiet at a time like this, help will come from heaven to the Jews, and they will be saved, but you will die and your father's family will come to an end. Yet who knows—maybe it was for a time like this that you were made queen!"

5. **Queen Esther sent Mordecai a reply.**

   Esther 4:15-16 (page ____ in the Old Testament): Esther sent Mordecai this reply: "Go and get all the Jews in Susa together; hold a fast and pray for me. Don't eat or drink anything for three days and nights. My servant girls and I will be doing the same. After that, I will go to the king, even though it is against the law. If I must die for doing it, I will die."

Queen Esther obeyed God. The Jews were saved. God uses people who obey Him to carry out His plan of love. God meets special needs/emergencies through people who obey Him.

> Answer the following questions:

1. Has God used *someone* to help you with a special need/emergency?
   _____

2. Has God used *you* to help someone with a special need/emergency?
   _____

DAILY BIBLE READINGS—Read from the Bible in your language and from the Good News Bible/Sunday School Bible:

Sunday	1 Peter 3:8-9
Monday	1 Peter 3:10-12
Tuesday	1 Peter 3:13-16
Wednesday	1 Peter 4:8-10
Thursday	James 2:14-17
Friday	James 2:22-25
Saturday	1 John 3:18

Lesson 43

Mary Chose to Obey God

Memory Verse: Luke 1:38a (page _____ in the New Testament): "I am the Lord's servant," said Mary; "may it happen to me as you have said."

For thousands of years, God had promised to send someone to save His people. God chose a young woman named Mary to be the mother of the Promised One.

1. **God sent an angel with a message for Mary.**

    Luke 1:28 (page _____ in the New Testament): The angel came to her and said, "Peace be with you! The Lord is with you and has greatly blessed you!"

2. **Mary was troubled by the angel's message. The angel comforted her.**

    Luke 1:29-33 (page _____ in the New Testament): Mary was deeply troubled by the angel's message, and she wondered what his words meant. The angel said to her, "Don't be afraid, Mary; God has been gracious to you. You will become pregnant and give birth to a Son, and you will name Him Jesus; He will be great and will be called the Son of the Most High God. The Lord God will make Him a King, as His ancestor David was, and He will be the King of the descendants of Jacob forever; His kingdom will never end."

3. **Mary did not understand the angel's message.**

    Luke 1:34 (page _____ in the New Testament): Mary said to the angel, "I am a virgin. How, then, can this be?"

4. **The angel explained his message.**

    Luke 1:35 (page _____ in the New Testament): The angel answered, "The Holy Spirit will come on you, and God's power will rest upon you. For this reason, the Holy Child will be called the Son of God."

God's Plan for Christian Living

5. Mary answered the angel.

Luke 1:38 (page _____ in the New Testament): "I am the Lord's servant," said Mary; "may it happen to me as you have said." And the angel left her.

6. Mary was happy because God chose her to be a part of His plan.

Luke 1:46-55 (page _____ in the New Testament): Mary said, "My heart praises the Lord; my soul is glad because of God my Savior, for He has remembered me, His lowly servant! From now on all people will call me happy, because of the great things the Mighty God has done for me. His name is Holy; from one generation to another He shows mercy to those who honor Him. He has stretched out His mighty arm and scattered the proud with all their plans. He has brought down mighty kings from their thrones and lifted up the lowly. He has filled the hungry with good things and sent the rich away with empty hands. He has kept the promise He made to our ancestors, and has come to the help of His servant Israel. He has remembered to show mercy to Abraham and to all His descendants forever!"

God has a special plan for each person. God's plan is for each person to choose His way.

> Answer the following questions:

1. Have you chosen God's plan for your life? _____

2. If you have not chosen God's plan for your life, will you, today, choose God's plan of love?
   _____

3. Will you, today, choose to obey God? _____

DAILY BIBLE READINGS—Read from the Bible in your language and from the Good News Bible/Sunday School Bible:

Sunday	Luke 1:5-7
Monday	Luke 1:8-10
Tuesday	Luke 1:11-14
Wednesday	Luke 1:15-17
Thursday	Luke 1:18-20
Friday	Luke 1:21-25
Saturday	Luke 1:26-28

Part V: The Christian Life—Growing through Obedience

Lesson 44

Jesus Called, the Fishermen Obeyed

Memory Verse: Matthew 4:22 (page ____ in the New Testament): Jesus called them, and at once they left the boat and their father, and went with Him.

When Jesus was about thirty years old, He began to tell people about God's love. He asked some people to help Him. The first people Jesus asked were fishermen: Peter, Andrew, James, and John.

Matthew 4:18-22 (page ____ in the New Testament): As Jesus walked along the shore of Lake Galilee, He saw two brothers who were fishermen, Simon (called Peter) and his brother Andrew, catching fish in the lake with a net. Jesus said to them, "Come with Me, and I will teach you to catch men." At once they left their nets and went with Him. He went on and saw two other brothers, James and John, the sons of Zebedee. They were in their boat with their father Zebedee, getting their nets ready. Jesus called them, and at once they left the boat and their father, and went with Him.

Jesus asked four fishermen to help Him. They were not people of high position. They were not wealthy. They were not well educated. They were ordinary people.

These ordinary people chose to obey Jesus. They followed Him. He taught them about God's love. They helped Jesus tell other people about God's love.

When you choose to obey Jesus . . .

- you say "yes" to Him. You follow Him.
- He teaches you.
- you tell other people about God's love!

139

DAILY BIBLE READINGS—Read from the Bible in your language and from the Good News Bible/Sunday School Bible:

Sunday	Matthew 4:18-22
Monday	Luke 5:1-3
Tuesday	Luke 5:4
Wednesday	Luke 5:5-8
Thursday	Luke 5:9-11
Friday	Mark 1:16-18
Saturday	Mark 1:19-20

Lesson 45

A Boy Who Obeyed

> *Memory Verse: Acts 3:6b (page _____ in the New Testament): "But I give you what I have."*

- Jesus taught people.
- Jesus helped people.
- Jesus healed people.

Jesus was tired. He went across Lake Galilee to rest. A large crowd followed Him. By late afternoon, the people were hungry. There was no food to eat.

John 6:5, 7-13 (page _____ in the New Testament):

v. 5: Jesus looked around and saw that a large crowd was coming to Him, so He asked Philip, "Where can we buy enough food to feed all these people?"

v. 7: Philip answered, "For everyone to have even a little, it would take more than two hundred silver coins to buy enough bread."

vv. 8-9: Another one of His disciples, Andrew, who was Simon Peter's brother, said, "There is a boy here who has five loaves of barley bread and two fish. But they will certainly not be enough for all these people."

v. 10: "Make the people sit down," Jesus told them. (There was a lot of grass there.) So all the people sat down; there were about five thousand men.

v. 11: Jesus took the bread, gave thanks to God, and distributed it to the people who were sitting there. He did the same with the fish, and they all had as much as they wanted.

> vv. 12-13: *When they were all full, He said to His disciples, "Gather the pieces left over; let us not waste a bit." So they gathered them all and filled twelve baskets with the pieces left over from the five barley loaves which the people had eaten."*

The boy was willing to give what he had for Jesus to use. In Jesus' hands, it became more than enough. The boy had a lunch. What do you have?

1. Yourself? _____

2. Your influence? _____

3. Your talents? _____

4. Your time? _____

5. Your money? _____

DAILY BIBLE READINGS—Read from the Bible in your language and from the Good News Bible/Sunday School Bible:

Sunday	Mark 6:30-32
Monday	Mark 6:33-34
Tuesday	Mark 6:35-37
Wednesday	Mark 6:38-39
Thursday	Mark 6:40-41
Friday	Mark 6:42-44
Saturday	Mark 6:45-46

Lesson 46

Paul Chose to Obey God

Memory Verse: Acts 26:19 (page   in the New Testament): "And so, . . . I did not disobey the vision I had from heaven."

Paul lived in the first century A.D. God used Paul to tell many people about His love for everyone. God used Paul to write letters to Christians. The letters told Christians God's plan for living.

Paul told how Jesus changed his life.

Acts 22:3-4, 6-8, 10-15 (page ____ in the New Testament):

v. 3: "I am a Jew, born in Tarsus in Cilicia, but brought up here in Jerusalem as a student of Gamaliel. I received strict instruction in the Law of our ancestors and was just as dedicated to God as are all of you who are here today."

v. 4: "I persecuted to the death the people who followed this Way. I arrested men and women and threw them into prison."

vv. 6-8: "As I was traveling and coming near Damascus, about midday a bright light from the sky flashed suddenly around me. I fell to the ground and heard a voice saying to me, 'Saul, Saul! Why do you persecute Me?' 'Who are You, Lord?' I asked. 'I am Jesus of Nazareth, whom you persecute,' He said to me."

v. 10: "I asked, 'What shall I do, Lord?' and the Lord said to me, 'Get up and go into Damascus, and there you will be told everything that God has determined for you to do.'"

vv. 11-13: "I was blind because of the bright light, and so my companions took me by the hand and led me into Damascus. In that city was a man named Ananias, a

God's Plan for Christian Living

religious man who obeyed our Law and was highly respected by all the Jews living there. He came to me, stood by me, and said, 'Brother Saul, see again!' At that very moment, I saw again and looked at him."

v. 14: "He said, 'The God of our ancestors has chosen you to know His will, to see His righteous Servant, and to hear Him speaking with His own voice."

v. 15: "For you will be a witness for Him to tell everyone what you have seen and heard.'"

Paul obeyed God. He told people about God's love. He started churches. He visited the churches. He wrote letters to the people in the churches. The letters told people how to live the Christian life.

Acts 26:19 (page _____ in the New Testament): "And so, King Agrippa, I did not disobey the vision I had from heaven."

Romans 1:1, 5-7 (page _____ in the New Testament): "From Paul, a servant of Christ Jesus and an apostle chosen and called by God to preach His Good News . . . . Through Him, God gave me the privilege of being an apostle for the sake of Christ, in order to lead people of all nations to believe and obey. This also includes you who are in Rome, whom God has called to belong to Jesus Christ. And so I write to all of you in Rome whom God loves and has called to be His own people: May God our Father and the Lord Jesus Christ give you grace and peace."

Paul's letters in the New Testament tell Christians God's plan for living the Christian life.

DAILY BIBLE READINGS—Read from the Bible in your language and from the Good News Bible/Sunday School Bible:

Sunday	Acts 9:1-2
Monday	Acts 9:3-6
Tuesday	Acts 9:7-9
Wednesday	Acts 9:10-12
Thursday	Acts 9:13-16
Friday	Acts 9:17
Saturday	Acts 9:18-20

Lesson 47

Jesus: The Perfect Example of Obedience

Memory Verse: John 3:16 (page _____ in the New Testament): For God loved the world so much that He gave His only Son, so that everyone who believes in Him may not die but have eternal life.

1. **Jesus lived in a human body. He obeyed His earthly parents.**

   Luke 2:51-52 (page _____ in the New Testament): So Jesus went back with them to Nazareth, where He was obedient to them. His mother treasured all these things in her heart. Jesus grew both in body and in wisdom, gaining favor with God and men.

2. **Jesus obeyed the law of His country.**

   Luke 20:21-25 (page _____ in the New Testament): These spies said to Jesus, "Teacher, we know that what You say and teach is right. We know that You pay no attention to a man's status, but teach the truth about God's will for man. Tell us, is it against our Law for us to pay taxes to the Roman Emperor, or not?" But Jesus saw through their trick and said to them, "Show Me a silver coin. Whose face and name are these on it?"

   "The Emperor's," they answered. So Jesus said, "Well, then, pay to the Emperor what belongs to the Emperor, and pay to God what belongs to God."

3. **Jesus obeyed God.**

   Matthew 26:38-39 (page _____ in the New Testament): He said to them, "The sorrow in My heart is so great that it almost crushes Me. Stay here and keep watch with Me." He went a little farther on, threw Himself face downward on the ground, and prayed, "My Father, if it is possible, take this cup of suffering from Me! Yet not what I want, but what You want."

4. **Jesus ALWAYS obeyed God.**

   Philippians 2:8 (page _____ in the New Testament): He was humble and walked the path of obedience all the way to death—His death on the cross.

God's Plan for Christian Living

Jesus was the perfect example of obedience. First, He obeyed His parents. He was all God, and He was all man. He had to learn from His parents. He learned that obeying His parents was important.

God wants children to obey parents today. When they obey parents, they learn to obey others in authority. Jesus is the perfect example for children today.

Jesus obeyed His parents. He obeyed the laws of His country. He obeyed the Jewish laws of God. He obeyed the laws of the Romans, who ruled the Jews. He taught others to obey also.

Our laws are made to protect the people. God's laws are given to teach us about Him. Jesus wants us to obey our laws and God's laws today.

Jesus obeyed God in all things. He is our perfect example of obedience.

Answer the following questions:

1. Did Jesus obey His parents? _____

2. Should children obey their parents today? _____

3. Did Jesus obey God? _____

4. Should YOU obey God? _____

5. Why should you obey God?

   _____

   _____

   _____

DAILY BIBLE READINGS—Read from the Bible in your language and from the Good News Bible/Sunday School Bible:

Sunday	Philippians 2:1-2
Monday	Philippians 2:3-4
Tuesday	Philippians 2:5-6
Wednesday	Philippians 2:7
Thursday	Philippians 2:8
Friday	Philippians 2:9
Saturday	Philippians 2:10-11

Lesson 48

Jesus: The Perfect Example of Obedience (Continued)

Memory Verse: Philippians 2:8 (page ____ in the New Testament): He was humble and walked the path of obedience all the way to death—His death on the cross.

Jesus ALWAYS obeyed God. One time when Jesus obeyed God, He could not obey His parents. Sometimes, when Jesus obeyed God, He could not obey the religious traditions of his people. Jesus ALWAYS obeyed God.

1. **When Jesus was a boy, He went with His parents to Jerusalem.**

    Luke 2:41-42 (page ____ in the New Testament): Every year the parents of Jesus went to Jerusalem for the Passover Festival. When Jesus was twelve years old, they went to the festival as usual.

2. **Jesus chose to stay in Jerusalem.**

    Luke 2:43-46 (page ____ in the New Testament): When the festival was over, they started back home, but the boy Jesus stayed in Jerusalem. His parents did not know this; they thought that He was with the group, so they traveled a whole day and then started looking for Him among their relatives and friends. They did not find Him, so they went back to Jerusalem looking for Him. On the third day they found Him in the Temple, sitting with the Jewish teachers, listening to them and asking questions.

3. **Jesus' parents found Him in the Temple.**

    Luke 2:47-48 (page ____ in the New Testament): All who heard Him were amazed at His intelligent answers. His parents were astonished when they saw Him, and His mother said to Him, "Son, why have You done this to us? Your father and I have been terribly worried trying to find You."

4. **Jesus chose to obey God.**

    Luke 2:49-50 (page ____ in the New Testament): He answered them, "Why did you have to look for Me? Didn't you know that I had to be in My Father's house?"

God's Plan for Christian Living

5. Jesus chose to return to Nazareth with His parents. He chose to obey His parents.

Luke 2:51-52 (page ____ in the New Testament): So Jesus went back with them to Nazareth, where He was obedient to them. His mother treasured all these things in her heart. Jesus grew both in body and in wisdom, gaining favor with God and men.

The great missionary, Paul, tells children to obey their parents. He tells parents to be kind to their children. He tells them to train their children according to the teachings of Jesus.

Ephesians 6:1-4 (page ____ in the New Testament): Children, it is your Christian duty to obey your parents, for this is the right thing to do. "Respect your father and mother" is the first commandment that has a promise added: "so that all may go well with you, and you may live a long time in the land." Parents, do not treat your children in such a way as to make them angry. Instead, raise them with Christian discipline and instruction.

Answer the following questions:

1. Why did Jesus disobey His parents?
   _____
   _____

2. Did you ever disobey your parents?
   _____
   _____

3. Why did you disobey?
   _____
   _____

DAILY BIBLE READINGS—Read from the Bible in your language and from the Good News Bible/Sunday School Bible:

Sunday	Luke 2:39-40
Monday	Luke 2:51-52
Tuesday	Matthew 12:1-4
Wednesday	Matthew 12:5-8
Thursday	Matthew 12:9-11
Friday	Matthew 12:12-14
Saturday	Matthew 12:15-18

Lesson 49

Jesus: The Perfect Example of Obedience (Continued)

Memory Verse: Philippians 2:8 (page _____ in the New Testament): He was humble and walked the path of obedience all the way to death—His death on the cross.

Jesus ALWAYS obeyed God. Sometimes when Jesus obeyed God, He could not obey the religious traditions of His people.

God gave His laws to His people. God's laws told the people to love God and to love people.

God's laws were good.

Religious leaders added many hard things to God's laws. Religious leaders added things the people could not understand. The added things became known as religious traditions. It was impossible for the people to learn all the religious traditions. The traditions became a burden to the people.

Jesus wanted people to know God's laws. He wants people to love God and to love people. Loving is helping.

1. **Jesus saw a man with a paralyzed hand. The man could not work. Jesus wanted to help the man.**

    Mark 3:1 (page _____ in the New Testament): Then Jesus went back to the synagogue, where there was a man who had a paralyzed hand.

God's Plan for Christian Living

2. **Some people wanted to accuse Jesus of doing wrong things. A religious tradition said, "Do not heal on the Sabbath."**

   Mark 3:2 (page ____ in the New Testament): Some people were there who wanted to accuse Jesus of doing wrong; so they watched Him closely to see whether He would cure the man on the Sabbath.

3. **Jesus wanted to help the man. He asked the people a question.**

   Mark 3:3-4 (page ____ in the New Testament): Jesus said to the man, "Come up here to the front." Then He asked the people, "What does our Law allow us to do on the Sabbath? To help or to harm? To save a man's life or to destroy it?" But they did not say a thing.

4. **The people wanted Jesus to keep the religious traditions. They did not want Him to heal the man's hand on the Sabbath day. Jesus was angry, but He loved the people. Jesus wanted to help the man. He loved the man. Loving is helping.**

   Mark 3:5 (page ____ in the New Testament): Jesus was angry as He looked around at them, but at the same time He felt sorry for them, because they were so stubborn and wrong. Then He said to the man, "Stretch out your hand." He stretched it out, and it became well again.

5. **The Pharisees were the religious leaders. They did not love people. They wanted people to keep the religious traditions. They thought that Jesus did bad things. They wanted to kill Him.**

   Mark 3:6 (page ____ in the New Testament): So the Pharisees left the synagogue and met at once with some members of Herod's party, and they made plans to kill Jesus.

Jesus ALWAYS obeyed God's laws. God's laws told people to love God and to love one another. Sometimes Jewish religious leaders forgot God's laws. Sometimes Jewish religious leaders made religious traditions more important than God's laws.

Sometimes Christians forget God's laws. Sometimes Christians make religious traditions more important than God's laws. God wants Christians to obey His laws.

> *Acts 5:29 (page ____ in the New Testament): Peter and the other apostles answered, "We must obey God, not men."*

Part V: The Christian Life—Growing through Obedience

Answer the following questions:

1. Why did Jesus disobey the Jewish religious traditions?

   _____

   _____

2. Why did Jesus heal the man on the Sabbath?

   _____

   _____

3. Would you obey religious traditions, or would you obey God?

   _____

   _____

DAILY BIBLE READINGS—Read from the Bible in your language and from the Good News Bible/Sunday School Bible:

Sunday	Hebrews 11:1-3
Monday	Psalm 33:6-9
Tuesday	John 1:1-5
Wednesday	Genesis 12:1-4
Thursday	Genesis 12:5-6
Friday	Genesis 12:7
Saturday	Genesis 12:8-9

Part VI:

The Christian Life—Living as God's Dear Children

Lesson 50

Living as God's Dear Children

> *Memory Verse: Ephesians 5:1-2 (page _____ in the New Testament): Since you are God's dear children, you must try to be like Him. Your life must be controlled by love, just as Christ loved us and gave His life for us as a sweet-smelling offering and sacrifice that pleases God.*

The New Testament contains thirteen letters written by Paul. These letters tell God's plan for the Christian life.

1. **You became one of God's dear children when you were born again.**

    Ephesians 1:13 (page _____ in the New Testament): And you also became God's people when you heard the true message, the Good News that brought you salvation. You believed in Christ, and God put His stamp of ownership on you by giving you the Holy Spirit He had promised.

2. **God gave you a new kind of life.**

    Ephesians 2:4-5 (page _____ in the New Testament): But God's mercy is so abundant, and His love for us is so great, that while we were spiritually dead in our disobedience, He brought us to life with Christ. It is by God's grace that you have been saved.

3. **God gives you the power to live the new kind of life.**

    Ephesians 1:19-20 (page _____ in the New Testament): How very great is His power at work in us who believe. This power working in us is the same as the mighty strength which He used when He raised Christ from death and seated Him at His right side in the heavenly world.

God's Plan for Christian Living

4. **God tells you how to live the new kind of life.**

    Ephesians 5:1 (page _____ in the New Testament): Since you are God's dear children, you must try to be like Him.

5. **You grow as one of God's dear children when you obey Him.**

    Ephesians 3:19-21 (page _____ in the New Testament): Yes, may you come to know His love—although it can never be fully known—and so be completely filled with the very nature of God. To Him who by means of His power working in us is able to do so much more than we can ever ask for, or even think of: to God be the glory in the church and in Christ Jesus for all time, forever and ever! Amen.

> Answer the following questions:

1. Are you one of God's dear children? _____

2. Do you know you have a new kind of life? _____

3. Do you know God's power in your life? _____

4. Is your life controlled by God's love? _____

DAILY BIBLE READINGS—Read from the Bible in your language and from the Good News Bible/Sunday School Bible:

Sunday	John 3:16
Monday	Ephesians 1:13-14
Tuesday	Ephesians 2:4-5
Wednesday	Ephesians 2:8-9
Thursday	Ephesians 3:19-20
Friday	Ephesians 4:22-24
Saturday	Ephesians 4:25-26

Part VI: The Christian Life—Living as God's Dear Children

Lesson 51

No More Lying!

> *Memory Verse: Ephesians 4:25 (page _____ in the New Testament): No more lying, then! Everyone must tell the truth to his fellow believer, because we are all members together in the body of Christ.*

God loves people. God wants the best way of life for people. The Bible tells us how to live as God's dear children. Throughout the Bible, God teaches people to tell the truth.

1. **God gave Moses a commandment (one of ten).**

    Exodus 20:16 (page _____ in the Old Testament): "Do not accuse anyone falsely."

2. **The writer of Proverbs said this about lying:**

    Proverbs 12:22 (page _____ in the Old Testament): The LORD hates liars, but is pleased with those who keep their word.

3. **Jesus said this about lying:**

    John 8:44b (page _____ in the New Testament): "From the very beginning he (the Devil) was a murderer and has never been on the side of truth, because there is no truth in him. When he tells a lie, he is only doing what is natural to him, because he is a liar and the father of all lies."

4. **Paul said this about lying:**

    Ephesians 4:25 (page _____ in the New Testament): No more lying, then! Everyone must tell the truth to his fellow believer, because we are all members together in the body of Christ.

    Colossians 3:9-10 (page _____ in the New Testament): Do not lie to one another, for you have put off the old self with its habits and have put on the new self. This is the new

157

God's Plan for Christian Living

being which God, its Creator, is constantly renewing in His own image, in order to bring you to a full knowledge of Himself.

Paul told people how to keep from lying:

Philippians 4:8 (page _____ in the New Testament): In conclusion, my brothers, fill your minds with those things that are good and that deserve praise: things that are true, noble, right, pure, lovely and honorable.

Answer the following questions:

1. Has someone told a lie about you? _____

2. Were you angry? _____

3. Were you sad? _____

4. What did you do? _____

   _____

5. Have you told a lie? _____

6. Have you told a lie about someone? _____

7. Did you ask for forgiveness? _____

DAILY BIBLE READINGS—Read from the Bible in your language and from the Good News Bible/Sunday School Bible:

Sunday	Ephesians 2:4-7
Monday	Ephesians 2:8-10
Tuesday	Ephesians 3:14-19
Wednesday	Ephesians 3:20-21
Thursday	Ephesians 4:1-3
Friday	Ephesians 4:4-6
Saturday	Ephesians 5:1-2

Lesson 52

Do Not Stay Angry

Memory Verse: Ephesians 4:26 (page _____ in the New Testament): If you become angry, do not let your anger lead you into sin, and do not stay angry all day.

God loves people. God wants the best way of life for people. In the Old Testament God teaches about anger.

1. **The writer of Psalms said this about anger:**

   Psalm 37:8 (page _____ in the Old Testament): Don't give into worry or anger; it only leads to trouble.

   Psalm 37:1-7 (page _____ in the Old Testament): Don't be worried on account of the wicked; don't be jealous of those who do wrong. They will soon disappear like grass that dries up; they will die like plants that wither. Trust in the Lord and do good; live in the land and be safe. Seek your happiness in the Lord, and He will give you your heart's desire. Give yourself to the Lord; trust in Him, and He will help you; He will make your righteousness shine like the noonday sun. Be patient and wait for the Lord to act; don't be worried about those who prosper or those who succeed in their evil plans.

2. **The writer of Proverbs (Solomon) said this about anger:**

   Proverbs 14:17 (page _____ in the Old Testament): People with a hot temper do foolish things; wiser people remain calm.

   Proverbs 15:1 (page _____ in the Old Testament): A gentle answer quiets anger, but a harsh one stirs it up.

   Proverbs 21:14 (page _____ in the Old Testament): If someone is angry with you, a gift given secretly will calm him down.

   Proverbs 27:4a (page _____ in the Old Testament): Anger is cruel and destructive.

   Proverbs 29:22 (page _____ in the Old Testament): People with quick tempers cause a lot of quarreling and trouble.

God's Plan for Christian Living

3. The writer of Ecclesiastes said this about anger:

Ecclesiastes 7:9 (page _____ in the Old Testament): Keep your temper under control; it is foolish to harbor a grudge.

Ephesians 4:26 (page _____ in the New Testament): If you become angry, do not let your anger lead you into sin, and do not stay angry all day.

Answer the following questions:

1. What makes you angry?
   _____

2. What do you do when you are angry?
   _____

3. Does your anger make you cruel and destructive?
   _____

4. Have you done foolish things because of your hot temper?
   _____

5. Do you cause a lot of quarreling and trouble because of your quick temper?
   _____

6. How do you control your temper?
   _____

7. How do you control your anger?
   _____

Part VI: The Christian Life—Living as God's Dear Children

> Fill in the blanks with the missing words:

Trust in the Lord and do _____; . . . Seek your _____ in the Lord, and He will give you your _____ _____. Give _____ to the Lord; _____ in Him, and He will _____ you. . . . Be _____ and _____ for the Lord to act; . . . —*Psalm 37:3-7a (page ____ in the Old Testament)*

It is _____ to harbor a grudge. —*Ecclesiastes 7:9b (page ____ in the Old Testament)*

DAILY BIBLE READINGS—Read from the Bible in your language and from the Good News Bible/Sunday School Bible:

Sunday	Psalm 40:1-3
Monday	Psalm 40:4-5
Tuesday	Psalm 40:6-8
Wednesday	Psalm 40:9-11
Thursday	Psalm 92:1-4
Friday	Psalm 93
Saturday	Psalm 95:1-7

Lesson 53

Do Not Stay Angry (Continued)

Memory Verse: Ephesians 4:26 (page _____ in the New Testament): If you become angry, do not let your anger lead you into sin, and do not stay angry all day.

God loves people. God wants the best way of life for people. In the New Testament God teaches about anger.

1. **Jesus said this about anger:**

   Matthew 5:21-24 (page _____ in the New Testament): "You have heard that people were told in the past, 'Do not commit murder; anyone who does will be brought to trial.' But now I tell you: whoever is angry with his brother will be brought to trial. Whoever calls his brother 'You good-for-nothing!' will be brought before the Council, and whoever calls his brother a worthless fool will be in danger of going to the fire of hell. So if you are about to offer your gift to God at the altar and there you remember that your brother has something against you, leave your gift there in front of the altar, go at once and make peace with your brother, and then come back and offer your gift to God."

2. **Paul said this about anger:**

   Ephesians 4:31-32 (page _____ in the New Testament): Get rid of all bitterness, passion, and anger. No more shouting or insults, no more hateful feelings of any sort. Instead, be kind and tender-hearted to one another, and forgive one another, as God has forgiven you through Christ.

3. **James tells us what to do about anger:**

   James 1:19-20 (page _____ in the New Testament): Remember this, my dear brothers! Everyone must be quick to listen, but slow to speak and slow to become angry. Man's anger does not achieve God's righteous purpose.

Think about it…

　i.　How do you feel when you are angry?

　ii.　How do you feel when someone is angry with you?

　iii.　How do you deal with anger?

　iv.　Is there ever a right time to be angry?

> *Romans 12: 17-21 (page _____ in the New Testament): If someone has done you wrong, do not repay him with a wrong. Try to do what everyone considers to be good. Do everything possible on your part to live in peace with everybody. Never take revenge, my friends, but instead let God's anger do it. For the Scripture says, "I will take revenge, I will pay back, says the Lord." Instead, as the Scripture says: "If your enemy is hungry, feed him; if he is thirsty, give him a drink; for by doing this you will make him burn with shame." Do not let evil defeat you; instead, conquer evil with good.*

DAILY BIBLE READINGS—Read from the Bible in your language and from the Good News Bible/Sunday School Bible:

Sunday	Romans 12:1-2
Monday	Romans 12:3
Tuesday	Romans 12:4-5
Wednesday	Romans 12:6-8
Thursday	Romans 12:9-13
Friday	Romans 12:14-16
Saturday	Romans 12:17-21

Lesson 54

God Will Help You

Memory Verse: 1 Thessalonians 5:16-18 (page _____ in the New Testament): Be joyful always, pray at all times, be thankful in all circumstances. This is what God wants from you in your life in union with Christ Jesus.

Does God help you overcome anger? Yes, God helps you overcome anger. God helps you forgive. God helps you overcome bad things.

God helped Paul when bad things happened to him. Paul was beaten eight times. He was put in prison. He was shipwrecked. He was robbed. He was stoned. Many times he was without food, water, clothing, and sleep.

Paul's friends turned against him. They criticized him. Paul's enemies lied about him. They accused him falsely.

1. **Paul was in Philippi. Silas, his helper, was with him. Their enemies lied about them. They accused Paul and Silas falsely.**

    Acts 16:20-21 (page _____ in the New Testament): They brought them before the Roman officials and said, "These men are Jews, and they are causing trouble in our city. They are teaching customs that are against our law; we are Roman citizens, and we cannot accept these customs or practice them."

2. **The enemies of Paul and Silas did every bad thing to them.**

    Acts. 16:22-24 (page _____ in the New Testament): And the crowd joined in the attack against Paul and Silas. Then the officials tore the clothes off Paul and Silas and ordered them to be whipped. After a severe beating, they were thrown in jail, and the jailer was ordered to lock them up tight. Upon receiving this order, the jailer threw them into the inner cell and fastened their feet between heavy blocks of wood.

3. **Paul and Silas praised God. God helped them overcome bad things. God gave them victory.**

    Acts 16:25 (page _____ in the New Testament): About midnight Paul and Silas were praying and singing hymns to God, and the other prisoners were listening to them.

Part VI: The Christian Life—Living as God's Dear Children

Paul and Silas did not feel like praising God. They were in pain. They were cold. They were not comfortable. They were miserable.

Paul and Silas knew that only God could help them. They praised God with singing and praying. God helped them. God gave them victory.

> *1 Thessalonians 5:16-18 (page ____ in the New Testament): Be joyful always, pray at all times, be thankful in all circumstances. This is what God wants from you in your life in union with Christ Jesus.*

Answer the following questions:

1. Have you ever praised God when bad things happened?
   _____

2. Did God help you?
   _____

3. Will you praise God when bad things happen to you?
   _____

4. Do you believe God will help you?
   _____

DAILY BIBLE READINGS—Read from the Bible in your language and from the Good News Bible/Sunday School Bible:

Sunday	Psalm 92:1-4
Monday	Psalm 93:1-5
Tuesday	Psalm 95:1-5
Wednesday	Psalm 96:1-3
Thursday	Psalm 96:4-6
Friday	Psalm 96:7-9
Saturday	Psalm 98:4-6

God's Plan for Christian Living

Lesson 55

Put on God's Armor

Memory Verse: Ephesians 6:13 (page _____ in the New Testament): So put on God's armor now! Then when the evil day comes, you will be able to resist the enemy's attacks; and after fighting to the end, you will still hold your ground.

God made us free to choose. When we do not choose God's way, we give the devil a chance to control our lives. When we choose God's way, the Holy Spirit controls our lives.

Ephesians 6:10-12 (page _____ in the New Testament): Finally, build up your strength in union with the Lord and by means of His mighty power. Put on all the armor that God gives you, so that you will be able to stand up against the Devil's evil tricks. For we are not fighting against human beings but against the wicked spiritual forces in the heavenly world, the rulers, authorities, and cosmic powers of this dark age.

When we choose God's way, He gives us help to fight the devil.

Ephesians 6:13 (page _____ in the New Testament): So put on God's armor now! Then when the evil day comes, you will be able to resist the enemy's attacks; and after fighting to the end, you will still hold your ground.

Paul uses a word picture to describe God's help. Paul tells us God's help is like a soldier's armor.

Soldier's Armor	God's Armor
Belt	Truth
Breastplate	Righteousness
Shoes	Readiness to share Good News
Shield	Faith

Helmet	Salvation
Sword	Word of God

> *Ephesians 6:14-17 (page _____ in the New Testament): So stand ready, with truth as a belt tight around your waist, with righteousness as your breastplate, and as your shoes the readiness to announce the Good News of peace. At all times carry faith as a shield: for with it you will be able to put out all the burning arrows shot by the Evil One. And accept salvation as a helmet and the Word of God as the sword which the Spirit gives you.*

> *Ephesians 6:18 (page _____ in the New Testament): Do all this in prayer, asking for God's help. Pray on every occasion, as the Spirit leads. For this reason keep alert and never give up; pray always for all God's people.*

Answer the following questions:

1. Who can wear God's armor?
   _____

2. Does God's armor help Christians?
   _____

3. How does God's armor help Christians?
   _____

4. Are you a Christian? _____

5. Do you wear God's armor? _____

DAILY BIBLE READINGS—Read from the Bible in your language and from the Good News Bible/Sunday School Bible:

Sunday	Hebrews 4:12-13
Monday	Romans 10:9-11
Tuesday	Romans 10:12-13
Wednesday	Romans 10:14-15
Thursday	Romans 10:16-17
Friday	Romans 5:1-2
Saturday	1 Thessalonians 5:8-11

God's Plan for Christian Living

Lesson 56

Thank You, God!

Memory Verse: 1 Thessalonians 5:18 (page ____ in the New Testament): Be thankful in all circumstances. This is what God wants from you in your life in union with Christ Jesus.

> *God gives many blessings to His children.*
>
> *God's dear children thank Him.*
>
> *God tells His children to be thankful in all circumstances.*

1. **God gives material blessings.**

   1 Chronicles 29:11-13 (page ____ in the Old Testament): You are great and powerful, glorious, splendid, and majestic. Everything in heaven is Yours, and You are king, supreme ruler over all. All riches and wealth come from You; You rule everything, by Your strength and power; and You are able to make anyone great and strong. Now, our God, we give You thanks, and we praise Your glorious name.

   - What are your material blessings?

     _____
     _____
     _____

   - Do you thank God for your material blessings?

     _____

Part VI: The Christian Life—Living as God's Dear Children

2. **God provides special people for you.**

    i. God made your family. God loves your family. God wants your family to love Him. God wants the people in your family to love each other.

    Ephesians 5:28 and 6:1 (page _____ in the New Testament): Men ought to love their wives just as they love their own bodies. A man who loves his wife loves himself. . . . Children, it is your Christian duty to obey your parents, for this is the right thing to do.

    ii. God provides friends for you.

    Proverbs 18:24 (page _____ in the Old Testament): Some friendships do not last, but some friends are more loyal than brothers.

    Philippians 1:3-4 (page _____ in the New Testament): I thank my God for you every time I think of you; and every time I pray for you all, I pray with joy.

    - Who are the special people in your life?

    _____
    _____
    _____

    - Do you thank God for the special people in your life?

    _____

    - Do you thank the special people in your life?

    _____

God tells His children to be thankful in all circumstances. It is easy to thank God when you have many material blessings. It is easy to thank God when you have a good family and good friends.

- Can you thank God when you do not have many material blessings?
- Can you thank God when you have problems with your family?
- Can you thank God when friends disappoint you?

You can choose to thank God in all circumstances.

DAILY BIBLE READINGS—**Read from the Bible in your language and from the Good News Bible/Sunday School Bible:**

Sunday	Exodus 15:2
Monday	Nehemiah 8:10
Tuesday	Psalm 18:1-3
Wednesday	Psalm 94:18-19
Thursday	Isaiah 41:10
Friday	Habakkuk 3:17-19
Saturday	1 Thessalonians 5:18

Lesson 57

Relationships

Memory Verse: Ephesians 5:21 (page _____ in the New Testament): Submit yourselves to one another because of your reverence for Christ.

> Christian submission means...
>
> loving God and letting Him control your life,
>
> loving people with God's kind of love
>
> ...your wife/husband,
>
> ...your children,
>
> ...your parents,
>
> ...your neighbor,
>
> and your enemies.

1. **Paul tells about God's kind of love in 1 Corinthians 13. Words, knowledge, or actions have no meaning without love.**

   1 Corinthians 13:1-3 (page _____ in the New Testament): I may be able to speak the languages of men and even of angels, but if I have no love, my speech is no more than a noisy gong or a clanging bell. I may have the gift of inspired preaching; I may have all knowledge and understand all secrets; I may have all the faith needed to move mountains—but if I have no love, I am nothing. I may give away everything I have, and even give up my body to be burned—but if I have no love, this does me no good.

2. **Paul defines God's kind of love.**

   1 Corinthians 13:4-8a (page _____ in the New Testament):

   > *LOVE is patient and kind;*
   >
   > *LOVE is not jealous or conceited or proud;*
   >
   > *LOVE is not ill-mannered or selfish or irritable;*
   >
   > *LOVE does not keep a record of wrongs;*
   >
   > *LOVE is not happy with evil, but is happy with truth.*
   >
   > *LOVE never gives up; and its faith, hope and patience never fail.*
   >
   > *LOVE is eternal.*

   Ephesians 5:22, 25, 33b (page _____ in the New Testament): Wives, submit yourselves to your husbands as to the Lord. . . . Husbands, love your wives just as Christ loved the church and gave His life for it. . . . Every husband must love his wife as himself, and every wife must respect her husband.

   Answer the following questions:

   1. Write what Christian submission means.

      _____

      _____

   2. How can you show God's kind of love to your wife/husband?

      _____

      _____

   3. Do you show God's kind of love to your wife/husband by . . .

      i. being patient and kind? _____

      ii. not being jealous or conceited or proud? _____

iii. not being ill-mannered or selfish or irritable? _____

iv. not keeping a record of wrongs? _____

v. not being happy with evil? _____

vi. being happy with the truth? _____

vii. never giving up? _____

viii. having faith, hope, and patience? _____

> *Ephesians 6:1-4 (page _____ in the New Testament): Children, it is your Christian duty to obey your parents, for this is the right thing to do. "Respect your father and mother" is the first commandment that has a promise added: "so that all may go well with you, and you may live a long time in the land." Parents, do not treat your children in such a way as to make them angry. Instead, raise them with Christian discipline and instruction.*

4. How can you show God's kind of love to your children/parents?

   _____
   _____

5. Do you show God's kind of love to your children/parents by . . .

   i. being patient and kind? _____

   ii. not being jealous or conceited or proud? _____

   iii. not being ill-mannered or selfish or irritable? _____

   iv. not keeping a record of wrongs? _____

   v. not being happy with evil? _____

   vi. being happy with the truth? _____

   vii. never giving up? _____

   viii. having faith, hope, and patience? _____

> *Matthew 22:37-40 (page _____ in the New Testament): Jesus answered, "Love the Lord your God with all your heart, with all your soul, and with all your mind." This is the greatest and the most important commandment. The second most important commandment is like it: "Love your neighbor as you love yourself." The whole Law of Moses and teachings of the prophets depend on these two commandments.*

God's Plan for Christian Living

> *Matthew 5:43-44 (page _____ in the New Testament): You have heard that it was said, "Love your friends, hate your enemies." But now I tell you: love your enemies and pray for those who persecute you, . . .*

6. How can you show God's kind of love to all people?

   _____
   _____

7. Do you show God's kind of love to all people by . . .

   i. being patient and kind? _____

   ii. not being jealous or conceited or proud? _____

   iii. not being ill-mannered or selfish or irritable? _____

   iv. not keeping a record of wrongs? _____

   v. not being happy with evil? _____

   vi. being happy with the truth? _____

   vii. never giving up? _____

   viii. having faith, hope, and patience? _____

Think about it . . .

- Who is my neighbor?
- Where does my neighbor live?
- What do I do when my neighbor is kind to me?
- What do I do when my neighbor is unkind to me?
- Who is my enemy?
- Do I have a personal enemy?
- How do I feel about my enemy/enemies?
- Can I love my enemy/enemies with God's kind of love?
- Do I love my enemy/enemies with God's love?

DAILY BIBLE READINGS—Read from the Bible in your language and from the Good News Bible/Sunday School Bible:

Sunday–Saturday: Every day this week, read 1 Corinthians 13:4-8. Instead of reading the word love, substitute your name. Read: "[your name] is patient and kind," etc.

www.ingramcontent.com/pod-product-compliance
Lightning Source LLC
Chambersburg PA
CBHW081232170426
43198CB00017B/2741